The Carolina Indian Frontier

David H. Corkran

TRICENTENNIAL BOOKLET NUMBER 6

Published for the South Carolina Tricentennial Commission
by the University of South Carolina Press
Columbia, South Carolina

First Edition
Published in Columbia, S. C., by the
University of South Carolina Press, 1970

Manufactured in the United States of America
By Vogue Press, Inc.

SECOND PRINTING, 1973

LIBRARY OF CONGRESS CATALOG CARD DATA:

Corkran, David H
   The Carolina Indian frontier [by] David H. Corkran.
[1st ed.] Columbia, S. C., Published for the South Carolina
Tricentennial Commission by the University of South Carolina
Press [1970]

   71 p. map. 22cm. (Tricentennial booklet no. 6)
   Bibliography: p. 70–71.

   1. South Carolina—History—Colonial period. 2. Indians of North
America—South Carolina. 3. Indians of North America—Wars. I.
Title. (Series: South Carolina Tricentennial Commission. Tricen-
tennial booklet no. 6)
F272.C8   975.7'02   79-120589
ISBN 0-87249-195-1   MARC

DAVID H. CORKRAN is doing independent research for a history of
the Iroquois Indians and a biography of the Little Carpenter
(Attakullakulla).

Contents

I

The Coastal Frontier

Indian relations were one of the most important aspects of South Carolina's colonial era. The dynamics of her economic needs and international position caused her to develop the greatest Indian empire in all the colonies. In one hundred years it expanded from the seacoast to the Mississippi River. From her position as the principal southern outpost against French and Spanish America and that of Charleston as an important seaport she reached tentacles deep into the heart of the Indian country.

At the opening of the European history in North America, about 15,000 Indians occupied the area of modern South Carolina. These were scattered peripherally along the Savannah River to the southwest, along the foothills of the mountains to the west and northwest, and along the seacoast. But south and west of the Savannah and west of the mountains lived more populous Indian nations which were to beckon the trader and adventurer.

The first European contacts were made with the seacoast Indians, the Cusabo and Winyah in the territory that became known as Chicora from the name of a somewhat mythical town somewhere inland. The Cusabos and Winyahs were agriculturalists, hunters, and fishermen, living in a few scattered towns on the bays and inlets. The largest town of

1

which a description is available was that on Edisto Island
where scattered thatch dwellings in cornfields surrounded a
huge circular clay and thatch council house. Before it an
avenue of trees shaded the village playground where the
elders played their stick and stone bowling game. Inside the
council house stood the chief's bench long enough to seat
the headman, his wife, and four councillors. About the circular walls ran benches sufficient to accommodate the entire
population of several hundred. Cusabo society, like all Indian
societies, was orderly, firmly based on convention and tradition to accommodate in loose freedom a home life of peace
which all the men as warriors were required to defend.
Though much of Indian life was the tilling of cornfields and
the pursuit of game, intertribal wars flourished. To maintain
the warrior cult all eastern and southern tribes cultivated
constant vendettas against near or remote tribes.

The first European intruders were Spanish fortune hunters
seeking estates, slaves, and gold. In 1521 Pedro de Quexós,
serving Lucas Vásquez de Ayllon, who desired to establish
a huge estate after the Spanish West Indian model, seized
140 Indians at Winyah Bay to be sold as slaves in the West
Indies. Among them was one who upon conversion to Chris-
tianity became known as Francisco de Chicora. Transported
to Spain Francisco de Chicora developed into an excellent
showman who regaled Spanish savants with tall tales of his
native land. In 1526 de Ayllon established a settlement on
the Carolina coast with a sizeable company. His colony, suf-
fering from food shortages, seized Indian corn, and the
Indians revolted, destroying his settlement. Many years
passed before the Spaniards again tried the Carolina coast.

However, in 1540, Hernando de Soto, marching overland

from Florida with 600 men in search of gold and empire, cut into the Carolina backcountry. Crossing the Savannah River in the neighborhood of Silver Bluff, he found the Indian village of Cofitachiqui. He seized the Indian queen to guide him and several score natives to carry his baggage and turned up country seeking fabled lands. In the hills and mountains he encountered the goldless Cherokees, many of whom he enslaved, and then turned south into Alabama and so out of Carolina history.

In 1562 the Cusabo befriended French freebooters who established a base at Beaufort Sound from which to harass the Spanish gold fleets. Four years later the Spaniards destroyed the French and with the help of the Cusabos built Fort San Felipe. Because of food shortages, Captain Juan Pardo was sent with part of the garrison up country to live off the natives. Pardo in his wanderings established posts of short duration among the Cherokee and among the Wateree on Wateree River. On the coast missionaries attempted to convert the Cusabos. But in 1576, the priests' efforts to stamp out native superstitions coupled with the garrison's repeated demands for Indian corn provoked a rebellion. The Spaniads, unable to cope with the Indians, abandoned the fort, and the Indians burned it. Three years later Menéndez Marqués, having reestablished Spanish power at Beaufort by building Fort San Marcos, marched against the Cusabos and defeated them. But his fort proved untenable in a hostile countryside and was soon abandoned. In 1582 the Spaniards returned and established Fort Catuso and the mission of Santa Elena (St. Helen). Both thrived on Indian labor and Indian food. But in 1585–1586 the oppressed Cusabos deserted, and the mission and fort had to be abandoned. The missionaries, however, had made a few converts and for the next seventy-five years occasionally visited Santa Elena.

By 1670 the English in more than a half century of coloniz-ing experience had discovered a new source of wealth among the Indians—the fur and deerskin trade. This enterprise required preserving the Indians and maintaining peace with them. However, the Cusabo had ceased being great hunters. The Westo Indians, who now occupied the Silver Bluff area of ancient Cofitachiqui, barred them from the upcountry hunting grounds. The Westo Indians appear to have been an Iroquoian enclave who by Iroquois methods had incor-porated conquered southern Indians into their tribe and after 1655 had been reinforced by Iroquoian Eries fleeing before the all-conquering Five Nations of the later New York area. The Eries, or Ricohicrians, had drifted down behind Virginia and had moved in upon the Westos. From a palisaded long house style of village they had developed a trade for fire arms with the Virginians at Occannechi Island on the Roa-noke. Grown accustomed to European goods, they needed extensive hunting grounds and, equipped with guns, they drove the Cusabo hunters from the upcountry. As they be-came increasingly hunters, they paid less attention to agri-culture and began raiding the Cusabo corn harvest. In 1669 they ruined the Cusabo village on Beaufort Sound.

Thus it was that in 1670 the hard pressed bow and arrow Cusabo welcomed the English who came to settle at Kiawah Bay. They readily granted the settlers lands and provided them with the corn that enabled the colony to survive the first year. Late in 1670 they rallied with the English to ward off a Spanish attack. However, friendship with the local Cusabo of Kiawah did not prevent an English quarrel with the Cusso village thirty miles up Ashley River. These Indians, perhaps enraged by a white man's murdering one of their tribesmen, raided the settlers' corn and hogs. In 1671, in the Stono War, the settlers disciplined the Cussos. The war saw the beginning of Indian slavery by the English. Indian prisoners were sold and transported out of the colony.

By 1673 the colony felt the sting of the Westos who had also now begun to raid settlers' corn and hogs. Colonists attacked the Westos and sent Captain Maurice Mathews to seek an anti-Westo alliance with the Issaw or Catawba Indians 200 miles up country near the junction of the Catawba and Wateree rivers. These moves brought speedy peace. By 1674 Dr. Henry Woodward had opened a Charleston trade with the Westos. The peculiarity of this trade was that it dealt not only in deer and beaver skins, but also in Indian slaves. As the best armed of southern Indians the Westos had intimidated all the Indians of the southeast, warring effectively on the Cusabos, Yamasees, Creeks, Cherokees, and Catawbas from which they took numerous prisoners whom they sold to the Charleston slave trade. The colony regarded Woodward's alliance as having raised up an effective counter to Spanish efforts among the southeastern Indians. Though the Lords Proprietors had forbidden the enslavement of Indians save as colony prisoners of war, the traders sensing a big market both in the colony and abroad, subsidized the Westos in wars which became primarily slave raids. The decimation of the Cusabo which had already begun from white borne disease and rum continued at the hands of the Westos. Many a Cusabo bought from the Westos was sold by colonial slave traders in New York, New England, and the West Indies. However, in some grisly intrigue of the traders, perhaps over Westo trading debts, the Carolinians in 1680 made war on the Westos. They engaged neighbors of the Westos, newly arrived Shawnees from the west, to attack and bring down Westos for the slave trade. Creek Indians, with whom Woodward in 1670 had made a Carolina alliance, were invited to join the assault and share the profits. Pressed by hostile tribes on all sides and cut off from the Virginia and Carolina trade, the Westos abandoned their town and went north to join the Iroquois Five Nations.

On the coast, using a small quarrel as an excuse, the Carolinians enslaved most of the few Winyahs. The Cusabo declined rapidly and constituted but a few hamlets. Many became employees and hangers-on of the English. Others drifted into the uplands to amalgamate with the Siouian tribes of that region—the Peedees, Santees, Congarees, and Waterees. In 1712, in return for their services in the Tuscarora War, 250 of them were assigned a reservation on Paliwan Island, adjoining St. Helena's Island. By 1740 the once populous coastal tribes had disappeared. The Carolina Indian frontier had moved far to the west.

II

The Development of the West

The Cusabo decline and the elimination of the Westos had stripped Carolina not only of its lucrative Indian trade but also of its Indian barrier against Spanish Florida. For trade and protection it became necessary to find new Indian strength. To this end Dr. Henry Woodward was sent in 1685 with a long pack train of Indian goods to the Creek town of Cussita on the Chattahoochee. The Creeks welcomed the overture and became active trading allies of Carolina. A second ally arose out of the war of the Yamasee Indians of Florida with the Timuca Indians under Spanish protection. The Yamasees, who had once lived near the Spanish mission in Guale (Georgia), had been induced by the Spaniards to move to St. Augustine. There they had become embroiled with the local Timucas and had between 1680 and 1685 marched off to the Creek country. Lord Cardross, leader of the Scottish settlers at Port Royal, lured the Yamasees to settle between Port Royal and the Savannah River where they could be supplied by the English while they warred on the Timucas and held the Spanish allied Indians at bay. Cardross was suspected of having made this move in order to use the Yamasee as slave hunters in Florida. A thousand Yamasees established a dozen towns between the Combahee and Savannah rivers from which they enjoyed a brisk trade

7

with Port Royal and Charleston. For deerskins and slaves the Indians received woolens, axes, pots, kettles, hoes, guns, ammunition, and decorative sundries. In 1707 Carolina made their region the first Indian reservation in South Carolina.

More significant, however, was the Creek trade. The Creeks numbered between seven and eight thousand people established in sixty villages on the Chattahoochee, Tallapoosa, and Coosa rivers in what is now western Georgia and eastern Alabama. These villages generally consisted of several score single-family clay houses grouped on streets about a central square which held council arbors and a temple. Nearby on the flats stretched the cornfields. Some towns such as Coweta on the Chattahoochee and Tuckabatchee on the Tallapoosa held eight or nine hundred people. The Creek towns formed a loose confederacy, prestigiously headed at this time by the headman of Coweta, whom the Carolinians called "the Emperor."

The immediate effect of the English trade penetration into the Creek country was to extend Carolina influence into western Alabama. By 1686 the Tallapoosa Creeks were warring on the neighboring Choctaws to obtain prisoners for the Carolina slave markets. Shortly all the tribes westward to the Mississippi River felt the force of the Creeks' newly acquired guns. To the south the Creeks threatened the Spanish Apalachee missions of West Florida. The Spaniards replied with force and diplomacy in an attempt to obtain Creek recognition of Spanish sovereignty and to halt the English trade. Since Carolina lacked military power the Creeks accepted Spanish overlordship but continued their English trade. Spain was not a great trading nation and did not encourage Spanish traders to enter the Creek country.

When in 1689 the Spaniards built a fort at Apalachicola in
the Lower Creek country, most of the Lower Creeks moved
eighty miles to the eastward to Ockmulge to escape the
Spanish grip and continue the English trade. Providing the
Carolinians with heavy packs of deerskins and coffles of
Indian slaves, the Creeks grew rich in cotton and woolen
garments, hoes, axes, guns, ammunition, pots, kettles, and
the decorative sundries of beads, brass wire, and ornamental
bells. Though their Indian institutions remained, their dress
changed to a barbaric adaptation of European materials and
articles. Their hunting and agriculture became easier and
more extensive, and their warfare the most productive in
their history.

However, with the development of the Carolina trade the
Indians became economic slaves. The traders operated on
Charleston credit from which they outfitted Indian hunters
on credit to be repaid in deerskins and slaves. The Indian
appetite for goods and rum and the traders' greed plunged
the Indians into debts beyond their capacity to pay. Pressed
by their Charleston creditors, the traders in efforts to collect
abused the Indians. They beat debtors and even seized them
or members of their families to be sold. The Indians toler-
ated these excesses because they had nowhere else to turn
for goods, implements, rum, and weapons.

By 1690 from the Upper Creeks the traders had penetrated
into the Chickasaw country near present Memphis, Tennessee, and northward to the Cherokees in the mountains. But
at this time neither of these tribes became important in the
Carolina trade, for they were limited in their hunting by
Creek hostility to the south and the attacks of the Iroquois
from the north.

Nor did the Carolinians have an extensive trade to the
north. In the late seventeenth century, Virginians monopo-
lized the trade of the Catawbas. A small trade developed
with the Sewee, Santee, Congaree, and Wateree, but it did
not grow, since these tribes, perhaps never large, dwindled
rapidly after their contacts with English diseases and rum.
The Sewees being nearest the coast suffered the most. From
an overzeal for trade, they determined early to have a direct
trade with Europe. To this end they outfitted a fleet of dug-
out canoes with mats for sails and embarked two hundred
of their men to cross the ocean. Caught in a storm, half of
them drowned. Most of the survivors were picked up at sea
by an English ship and sold as slaves in the West Indies. By
1700 the Sewee numbered less than fifty people.

By 1701 the Creek involvement in the English trade
brought on a war with the Apalachee Indians of West Florida
which threatened to involve the English. Creeks had been
in the habit of buying Spanish horses from the Apalachees
which they then sold to the traders at a large profit. Inspired
by the Spaniards who wished to obtain more English goods
the Apalachees raised the price of horses. The infuriated
Creeks, backed by the Carolinians, then undertook horse
raids. The Spaniards supported the Apalachees and the Creeks
took on the Spaniards. In 1702 the Lower Creeks stormed
the Apalachee mission town of Santa Fe, burned it, and took
several score Apalachees prisoner whom they sold to the
English as slaves. The traders not only profited from the
slaves but from the increased sale of guns and ammunition.

A Creek-Choctaw war developed from the slave trade. By
1701 the French, having arrived on the gulf coast to establish
the Biloxi-Mobile settlements, discovered all the Indians of

the region terrorized by slave raiding Creeks. Grasping the opportunity to obtain allies against English pretensions in the area, they gave the Choctaws guns and the Choctaws immediately struck the Upper Creeks. The war forced the Creeks to even greater dependence upon the Carolina traders, ready as ever to supply guns and ammunition. However, since there was menace in the French lodgement on the gulf, the traders became more considerate of their Creek allies and eased their abuse of Creek debtors.

When in 1702 England went to war with Spain and France, the Carolinians used the Creeks in attempts to conquer Spanish Florida. In 1703 Colonel James Moore with Carolinians and a large force of Creeks, Yamasees, Cusabos, and Santee River Indians attacked St. Augustine, routed the Spanish Indians, burned the Indian settlements and mission town, and penned the Spaniards into the fort. When the Spaniards refused to surrender, Moore, unprepared for a siege, withdrew taking a long train of Indian captives to be sold in the slave mart. That same year Moore with fifty Carolinians and over a thousand Creeks assaulted the Apalachee missions, burned them, captured Fort St. Louis, and took hundreds of Apalachees prisoner. Many of these were sold in Carolina, but most were resettled on the Savannah River (near future Augusta) out of Spanish reach and within the Carolina trading orbit.

Meanwhile the Creeks, angered at French support of the Choctaws and rallied by the Carolina traders, carried on intermittent warfare against French Biloxi and Mobile. Inspired by the traders they made an alliance with the Chickasaws. In 1707 and 1708 the Creeks attacked newly built Spanish Pensacola and burned the town. In 1711 Carolinians led the Creeks under Emperor Brims of Coweta against the Choctaws in a highly successful campaign.

As the hostility of the Creeks toward the French and Spaniards rose, the traders became emboldened to exert more pressure in the collection of debts. As a result the Creeks made peace with their enemies. However, the Creeks could not throw off the traders, for the French and Spaniards could not supply them with the goods upon which they were dependent, and they continued to pile up debt. They helped Price Hughes to open up an extensive trade with the Chickasaws whom they wished to keep as allies to check the Choctaws. On behalf of the Carolina slave trade the Chickasaws raided the trans-Mississippi Indians.

Despite its drawbacks, the Carolina trade had raised Carolina's prestige high among the Indians. When in September 1711 the Tuscarora Indians of North Carolina, agitated by white land grabs, broke out into war, South Carolina raised hundreds of Indian allies to aid her defenseless neighbor. Late in the year Carolinian Colonel John Barnwell with Creeks, Yamasees, Catawbas, and others, marched from the Catawba River against the Tuscarora towns and waged an inconclusive campaign. Early in 1713 a second South Carolina expedition under Colonel James Moore, Jr., with over five hundred Cherokees, Creeks, and Catawbas went against the main Tuscarora fort of Nooherooka. On March 20, 1713, whites and Indians stormed the place and in fierce battle broke the Tuscarora power. Most of the surviving Tuscaroras retired to the north to join the Iroquois Five Nations, carrying with them hatred for the southern Indians who had fought them.

The period 1711 to 1713 saw the consolidation of the

farthest west penetration of the Carolina trade, that to the
Chickasaws. In a long see-saw of intrigue and counter intrigue
involving the French and Choctaws, Carolina agents Price
Hughes and Thomas Nairne developed great influence among
the Chickasaws, who now began to raid the French dom-
inated Illinois country for slaves for the Carolina market.
Though many of the more distant Indians were domiciled
as slaves in Carolina, great numbers were sold out of the
province. They made good workers and never threatened
revolt because Indians passively accepted captivity in alien
tribes with whom they expected eventually to be incor-
porated. In 1708 over eight hundred Indians worked as
slaves in Carolina.

Between 1708 and 1715 the Cherokees came into prom-
inence in the Carolina trade. They were a considerable
people settled in sixty towns and having at least five thousand men. The towns were in three groupings described by
the Carolinians as the Lower, Middle, and Upper Cherokees.
The Lower Cherokees comprised some twenty villages on
the headwaters of the Savannah and the Chattahoochee. Of
these the easternmost lived on Keowee River in present-day
Oconee County centering about the town of Keowee. Others
lived on the Toogaloo and Chatuga rivers which took their
names from Cherokee towns and westward to the headwaters of Chattahoochee where Nacoochee was an important
town. The Middle Settlements lay along the upper reaches
of the Little Tennessee in what are now Macon, Haywood,
and Swain counties in North Carolina. The larger towns
were Tassiche, Nequassee, Cowee, and Joree on the Little
Tennessee. Beyond were the Upper Cherokees or Overhills
who fell into two divisions, the Valley Towns including

Hiwassee, Euphase, and Quanasee on Hiwassee River, and the Overhills proper, beyond the mountains in what is now Monroe County, Tennessee. Their principal towns were Tanase-Chota and Settico.

The towns sat on flat lands beside rapidly moving rivers against a background of blue mountains. They consisted of scattered single-family, one-storied, clay and thatch houses set in cornfields. Near the river in the midst of ceremonial and gaming fields stood a large domelike council house which was the governmental and social center. Its circular benches could seat two or three hundred people. In each town the maintenance of civil decency lay in the hands of a "peace" or civil chief, assisted by clan headmen and war chiefs. These constituted the council which met on call to debate affairs. The principal councils were those of the "mother" towns, such as Great Tellico, Tanase, Ketuah, and Keowee, so called because they may have been the original towns of their groupings, but more likely because they happened by the accident of residence to be the hometowns of the heredity "oukas," or principal peace headmen, called by the Carolinians "kings." The most prestigious of all the "oukas" was generally the first man of Overhill Tanase-Chota. In the background of all councils moved the shadowy figures of priests and conjurers.

Cherokee town life was peaceful, and if the food supply held up, quite agreeable. Custom and tradition supported by taboo rather than law governed daily life. The routine was of household, cornfield, and seasonal hunts—punctuated by seasonal festivals, the principal of which was the green corn dance in late August or early September. War was a constant factor; for it formed a traditional part of a young man's growth and education. It necessitated far ranging vendettas. Great cataclysmic war was a rarity until the eighteenth-century embroilments generated from the English imperial and trading complexes. However, before these the Cherokees suffered from Westo slave raids and from the adventuring, glory-seeking Iroquois of the north.

The first recorded Cherokees to appear in Charleston were captives of one of the Savannah River tribes—presumably Shawnees in the slaving business—in the year 1681. In 1690 Captain James Moore explored the Appalachians with Cherokee guides. Very likely by then the Cherokees had been visited by Virginia traders and adventurers from Occonnechi post. In 1691 there was a report of Carolinians having murdered some Cherokees. In 1693 twenty Cherokee chiefs visited Charleston to complain to Governor Thomas Smith of attacks by the Catawba and Congaree Indians and of Shawnees who made outrageous slave raids. The trade with them was not great; in 1708 the Carolina council reported to the proprietors that the "trade we have with these people is inconsiderable, they being but ordinary hunters and less warriors."

A few years later the Carolina traders Eleazer Wiggan and Alexander Long had developed ties with the Cherokees from Long's trading post at the Yuchi town of Chestowe in northern Georgia. These two were well known to the Overhill head warrior—The Partridge. They enlisted many warriors in Colonel Barnwell's 1712 expedition against the Tuscaroras. Late in 1712 Cherokee dissatisfaction over trade matters caused the Carolina Commissioners of Indian Trade to send Thomas Nairne and John Wright to settle their grievances.

One of these grievances concerned a Cherokee of note, known to the English by the slave name of "Caesar." Caesar, taken as a youth by an enemy, had been for several years the slave of Carolina trader John Stephens at the Shawnee town. He had been induced by one of his countrymen, the headman Flint, to run off to the Cherokee country. Stephens seized Flint's goods and ominous Indian talk followed. From such incidents Indian war could arise. The Cherokees finally agreed to reimburse Stephens for Caesar on return of Flint's goods, and Caesar thereby became a free man in the Middle Settlements town of Watoga where, as the one Cherokee who could speak English well, he exercised great influence. He seems never to have resented his enslavement, and throughout his career, which lasted into the sixties when he was headman of Overhill Chatuga, he remained a firm friend of the English.

In 1713 Overhill Cherokees under The Partridge of Tanase at the behest of Alexander Long and Eleazer Wiggan raided Yuchi Chestowe and took prisoners to be sold as slaves to pay Yuchi debts to the two traders. The Carolina government reacted to this barbarity by summoning Long and Wiggan to Charleston. Wiggan was cleared, but Long fled from Carolina wrath to the Overhill Cherokee country where he spread stories that Carolina would surely attack the Cherokees for their part in the Chestowe affair. At that time Cherokee trade with Carolina was growing. At the urging of Carolina agent Price Hughes they undertook to bring the Illinois Indians into alliance and trade with Carolina. Numbers of Carolina traders operated in the Cherokee nation and half the Cherokee warriors had guns.

North from the Congarees up the Wateree on Catawba

River lived the Catawba Indians in present York and Lancaster counties. In the late seventeenth century they numbered perhaps 2,000 and later as they dwindled were to recruit to themselves the nearby Waxhaws, Waterees, Congarees, Santees, and related small tribes. Of Siouian stock, they inhabited a few villages very much like other southeastern Indian villages—scattered single-family houses in the cornfield flats centering on a council house by the river. Since at least 1662 they had been in the Virginia trading orbit, at first making the long trek to the Occonnechi post on Roanoke and after 1670 being the objective of Virginia packhorse convoys. Since 1679 they had been raided by the northern Five Nations Iroquois. It was a vendetta engendered by wanton war mongering and lasted almost to the American Revolution.

Early Carolina contacts with the Catawbas are shadowy. There is a story that in 1670 the Catawbas, learning of the approach of William Sayle's fleet to settle Charleston, sent a war party to have a surreptitious look. This is possible because, having become accustomed to white men's trading goods out of Virginia, they would be interested in a new trading center which might provide goods more cheaply. In 1671 Henry Woodward on an overland trip from Charleston to Virginia may have passed through their country. By then the Carolina settlers were aware of the Catawbas, for in August Maurice Mathews listed them as one of the tribes "in trade and friendship" with Carolina. In the autumn of 1673 the Council sent Mathews and several others to enlist the Catawbas against the Westos. However, their trade was slow to develop; in 1692 Carolina still regarded them as strangers to be eagerly cultivated. In June 1692 the Grand

Council of South Carolina declared all Indians within 400
miles of Charleston under the colony's protection. The pro-
tectorate was designed to extend Carolina law over the traders
in remote places rather than to make the Indians subjects
of the crown. But by 1701 the Charleston traders Stephen
Bull and Robert Fenwick were pressing the colony government to make the Catawbas more dependent on Carolina.
This request was probably directed at the Virginia trade.
By then the Catawbas had come into some sort of subjection
to Carolina; in January of that year the adventurer John
Lawson found they had orders from Carolina to deliver ten
deer skins to Governor James Moore in tribute.

Lawson out of curiosity had journeyed with traders from
Charleston up the Santee River, through cypress swamps and
winter flooded valleys, past the Santee village with its scattered cornfields and mounds (Nelson's Ferry), on to the
small Congaree village (near Columbia) much reduced by
wars and smallpox, through the cane brakes up the Wateree,
to the Waxhaws and Catawbas. He found the Catawbas
cherishing horses they had obtained from Virginia. After a
few days' journey further north he turned eastward to the
North Carolina coast. Throughout the trip at the Indian
villages his companions were "entertained" by the Indian
girls, some of them operating as "trading girls" under the
auspices of headmen who collected their fees. Now and then
one proved light-fingered and unofficially collected for her-
self from her mate for the night.

By 1707 the Carolinian William Canty was active in the
Catawba trade. In that year he brought a party of Catawbas
to Charleston bearing gifts for the governor. By then Carolina had determined to enforce her sovereignty over the

Catawba country and to break up the Virginia trade. The
assembly passed laws enforcing the collection of export
duties on deerskins taken from Carolina licenses. Colony
agents in the Catawbas seized the goods of Virginia traders
causing an intercolonial hassle which ended a year or two
later in the crown's disallowing the Carolina laws.

By 1711 the Carolina-Catawba trade had grown to the
extent that the Catawbas complained of the usual abuses—
faulty weights and measures and brutal efforts to collect
rum debts. The colony sent agent John Wright to redress
grievances. Wright placated the Catawbas, and they joined
heartily in Barnwell's fall expedition against the Tuscaroras.
In the assault upon Fort Nahrontes they behaved valiantly,
but like most of the Indians they left after the action to go
home and sing their exploits and scalps taken. In 1713, led
by Captain John Canty, they distinguished themselves in the
assault on Fort Nooherooka. They took numerous Tuscarora
prisoners whom they sold to the Carolinians. A product of
the Catawba-Tuscarora enmity was a renewal of the war
with the northern Iroquois allies of the Tuscaroras, which
was signalized in 1713 by the Catawba murder of Mohawk
envoys. The Iroquois remembered with vengeance for many
years.

III

The Yamasee War and Its Aftermath

Between 1712 and 1713, though the Carolina trade prospered, the Indians did not. They were goods hungry, and the impact of the trade had altered their economy into a dependence upon European arms, utensils, and clothing. They had also developed an appetite for rum. Rum freed them from the tension of Indian life regulated by rigid custom and taboo. The Indians regarded an intoxicated man as out of his senses and not punishable for the excesses he committed. A drunken Indian could therefore unshackle his private grudges against his fellows or wife and children without fear of reprisal—and many a murder occurred in drunken orgies. They also enjoyed drunkenness and with whoops and howls indulged in the wildest of excesses. So great was their appetite for liquor that they readily went into debt to obtain it. Sometimes a village after a mass drunk sobered to find itself with a heavy debt, for when intoxicated they would set their marks to anything a trader presented. Headmen frequently protested the sale of liquor as destructive of Indian institutions, but as frequently asked that they themselves be exempted from any prohibition.

By 1715 the Indian debt to Carolina merchants was estimated at more than £50,000. Pressed by the merchants, the traders mercilessly collected from Indian debtors, some even seizing a debtor or his wife and children to be sold into slavery. By 1714 it began to appear to many Indians that the way out was to kill all the traders. War belts passed from the Creeks to the Cherokees, the Yamasees, and the Catawbas. The French and Spanish hand in this is obscure. The Yamasees, particularly hard pressed, took the lead by launching a surprise attack on April 11, 1715. All traders in the Yamasee and Creek country were murdered. Some of those among the Cherokees, protected by Indian friends, escaped, but most there and among the Catawbas died.

The Yamasees with scalping knife and fire swept through the plantations of the Port Royal area and into the town itself. They killed scores and took many prisoners before the survivors fled to a ship in the harbor. War flamed from the Savannah to the Santee. Governor Charles Craven launched a counter attack from Port Royal, and though nearly surrounded at a battle near the head of Combahee, he checked the Yamasees. Stockaded posts were hurriedly constructed on outlying plantations. To the north in June 400 Catawbas and Santees ambushed ninety whites advancing against them, the Carolinians barely being able to fight their way out with the loss of thirty. Finally on June 13 Captain George Chicken at the battle of Goose Creek fought from four in the afternoon until dark to drive the Indians back. Cherokees advanced from the northwest but finding support weak withdrew. In July 1,000 Creeks and Yamasees under the Lower Creek war chief Chigelley hovered on the outskirts of Charleston. Carolina by superhuman efforts rallied its remaining manpower, including Negro slaves, and repulsed the assault.

Fortunately for Carolina, Cherokee participation had not

been wholehearted. The Cherokees were divided. The trader
Eleazer Wiggan talked the Carolina council into allowing
him to negotiate a peace with the Cherokees. He brought
down to Charleston his friends, the Tanase warrior The Partridge and the ex-slave Caesar, who arranged for Carolina
troops to go to the Cherokee country to act against the
Creeks. In the autumn Colonel Maurice Moore led 300 Carolinians, including two companies of Negroes, to Toogaloo, the
town of Charite Hayge, the most prestigious of the Lower
Cherokees. Charite Hayge was a doubtful quantity for he
was related to the Yamasees. He had feelers out to the Creeks
which he represented as peace overtures, but which the
Creeks regarded as expressions of sympathetic understanding.
The Partridge· and Caesar, distrusting Charite Hayge, were
hot for war on the Creeks. The Creeks relying on Charite
Hayge sent deputies to Toogaloo to urge a massacre of the
English troops. Concealed in the woods a day's journey away
waited hundreds of Creek warriors. The Partridge and
Caesar murdered the Creek ambassadors and then with
Moore's forces surged out against the Creek warriors, who
quickly fled. Thus the Cherokees committed themselves to
the English as allies. They raided Creek towns and French
convoys on the Mississippi. With the Cherokees allies of the
English, the Creek and Yamasee positions became untenable.
The Yamasee attacked by Governor Craven fled to St. Augustine, and the Lower Creeks withdrew their towns from the
Ocmulgee River to the Chattahoochee. The Catawbas after
their June repulse decided to approach Virginia for a peace
which was concluded at Williamsburg.

The Creeks finding themselves alone in the war, granted
the French the right to build a fort in their country at the

junction of the Tallapoosa and Coosa. Fort Toulouse, always garrisoned by from twenty to forty men, was for nearly half a century to be a base of French influence in the Creek nation. Emperor Brims of Coweta stood on the defensive, while the Upper Creeks, short of ammunition and subject to Cherokee raids, began to think peace. All the Creeks felt the pinch of the cessation of the English trade. The French and Spaniards could not supply them. In this situation Brims listened in 1717 to Carolina envoys Theophilus Hastings and John Musgrove. Gradually a peace with renewal of trade was worked out. The Yamasees, however, now safe under the guns of St. Augustine, conducted sporadic raids against Carolina for another ten years despite Carolina attempts to force the Creeks to keep them quiet.

Carolina mended her trading ways. For a few years a government monopoly was carried on from government trading houses, the principal of which were at the Shawnee town above Silver Bluff and at the Congarees. The system did not please the Indians who before the war had traders coming into their towns. In 1720 private pressures and money losses put an end to the government monopoly and private trading companies were allowed to reenter the Indian country. But the colony had learned a lesson. Traders were prohibited from granting individual Indians more than fifty pounds credit, and the Indian slave trade was practically abolished. Traders became more circumspect in debt collection, and the rum trade was for a while restrained. To protect the Carolina western frontiers from Yamasee raids Fort Moore was established near the Shawnee town and further down the Savannah Fort Palachicola. Two ranger companies were assigned to border patrol. But Carolina faced a new situation in which the Creeks courted the Spaniards and the French. Emperor Brims had grasped the idea that he could play French and Spaniards against the English and thereby maintain Creek independence.

The principal Carolina Indian problem during the decade 1718–1728 was how to turn the Creeks against the Yamasee. Many Creeks, who were related to the Yamasee, could join with impunity Yamasee raiding parties. Carolina hoped by supporting the Cherokees against the Creeks to force the Creeks to beg for peace at Carolina's price. Carolina not only supplied the Cherokees with munitions but through the traders kept them informed of intended Creek attacks. Carolina also threatened the Creeks with trade embargoes. Negotiations see-sawed throughout the decade, and there were stern episodes, for the Creeks were acutely conscious of Carolina support of the Cherokees. In 1724 a Creek party under Upper Towns' Gogel Eyes, raiding the Cherokees, sacked the store of Toogaloo trader John Sharpe, and after wounding him carried off his goods and Negro slaves. Carolina sent Colonel Tobias Fitch to Brims to demand satisfaction and Colonel George Chicken to the Cherokees to urge more attacks on the Creeks. Fitch, with the cooperation of Upper Creek headmen, finally received from Brims a promise of indemnity and no further interference with the Cherokee trade. But Brims determined to destroy the Cherokees and refused to break with the Yamasee. When Yamasees, seeking to break Carolina intercourse with the Creeks, killed Brims' pro-English son Ouletta, Fitch's diplomacy seemed headed for success. Brims broke with the Yamasee and talked war. But Governor Benevides of Florida, desiring to prevent a Creek-Yamasee war, executed the murderers of Ouletta and sent their heads to Brims. He reminded Brims that the English had encouraged the Cherokees to war on the Creeks. When in 1726, 500 Cherokees bearing an English flag attacked the Lower Creeks, Brims decided to accept a Spanish alliance and go to war against Carolina. Upper Creeks frustrated him for they did not want their trade interrupted. Carolina also decided that matters had gone too far and that the Cherokee-Creek war must end. The result was a peace making at Charleston in January 1727 attended by Hobohatchey of the Abeika and Chigelley of Coweta and Cherokees headed by the Long Warrior of Tanase. The Creeks agreed to a clean break with the Yamasee.

Phasing out the Yamasee war seemed imminent. However, the Spaniards fomented an intrigue by which some Yamasees and their Creek relatives attacked the store of Carolina trader Smallwood on the Altamaha River and killed Smallwood and his men. Carolina planned an expedition against the Creeks, demanded indemnity, and declared a trade embargo on the Lower Creeks. Charlesworth Glover was sent to Coweta with an ultimatum and Colonel John Herbert was sent to the Cherokees to renew the Cherokee war against the Creeks if the Creeks did not come to terms. Brims was recalcitrant, but Glover managed to get Upper Creeks to take Yamasee scalps and to pressure Cherokeeleechee, an anti-English leader whose Apalachees occasionally joined Yamasee raiding parties, into promising to keep the peace. Carolina then sent Colonel John Palmer with 300 men against the Yamasees near St. Augustine and destroyed their town. Brims, perceiving Spanish impotence and the futility of supporting the Yamasee, agreed to a final break. Carolina lifted the trade embargo and recalled Herbert from the Cherokees.

Despite Carolina efforts to keep the Cherokees engaged against the Creeks in the period 1715–1727, the Cherokees were not always happy with the Carolinians. Most Cherokees were unwilling to go out either against the Creeks or the Yamasees unless Carolina maintained troops in their country. Carolina could not afford to do so. Cherokee raids on the Creeks were feeble, mostly led by faithful Caesar, who with The Partridge of Tanase and Charite Hayge maintained the English alliance. Cherokees were greatly distressed by Creek raids. The Cherokees were also unhappy with the trade. They objected to the long carry to Savanno town and the Congarees and forced Carolina to establish posts in some of their towns. These did not prosper. Late in 1717 the Virginia Trading Company sent a large convoy to the Cherokee country which sold goods at prices lower than Carolina could and which freed the Cherokees of the long twice-a-year carry to Charleston of the big bundles of deerskins the Carolina stores had taken. The state monopoly lost money, for the Cherokees now traded their prime skins to the Virginians and their second-rate skins to the Carolinians. They grew insolent to the Carolina traders. Fortunately for Carolina, the Virginia Company, opposed in Virginia as a monopoly, soon went out of business. Carolina promised to use horses instead of Indians for its pack trains, lost money on this program, and soon ended the state monopoly, reopening the Cherokee country to private traders. Charite Hayge had been killed by the Creeks in 1719 and the center of Carolina influence had shifted to Keowee. The efforts of private Virginians to enter the trade were thwarted by a new Carolina licensing act of 1721, and the Cherokees had to settle down into the hands of Carolina private traders.

Of growing concern to Carolina was possible French influence among the Cherokees. Since 1715 the Cherokees had been intermittently at war with the French Indians north of the Ohio. Occasionally they captured Frenchmen and brought them to their towns, and the Carolinians, fearful lest they corrupt the Indians with anti-English sentiments, always bought them. When in 1727 the Cherokees talked peace with the French-dominated Twightwees and Ottawas, Colonel Theophilus Hastings, then in the Cherokee country, attempted to prevent the talks but did not succeed. In 1728 as a result of the Cherokee-Creek peace, the French were able to put an agent in the Cherokee country; in 1729 the Creeks attempted to induce the Cherokees to open a trade with Fort Toulouse. Alarmed Carolina traders used every means to frustrate the overture. By 1729 the Cherokees had so much ill will toward the traders because of debts and other matters, that they listened to the French and discussed the possibility of war with the English.

In the spring of 1730 the situation changed dramatically. The psycopathic Englishman Sir Alexander Cuming, visiting the Cherokee country out of curiosity, learned of Cherokee unrest, and took action. Boldly he entered the Keowee town house and demanded that all fall on their knees and drink the king's health. Arriving at Tasseche in the midst of a violent thunderstorm he overawed the medicine man of that town with his apparent supernatural qualities. At Great Tellico he held council with the aspiring Moytoy and listened to his claims to the headship of the Cherokees. At Tanase he received the homage of the head warrior. Returning with a great entourage of warriors and headmen to Nequassee he witnessed the elevation of Moytoy to the emperorship and swore all to allegiance to England. As a result of these extravagant actions Cuming prevailed on the Cherokees to send six ranking deputies with him to England to see the king and make a treaty of alliance with the Crown. This treaty, guaranteeing the Cherokees a trade with any English colony which chose to send traders to them and subjecting the Cherokees to English overlordship, became the cornerstone of Cherokee-English relations for the next three decades. The Cherokees were occasionally to interpret it as meaning independence from the Carolina trade monopoly. Moytoy, whose elevation had occurred perhaps in revulsion to anti-English Tanase, remained as principal ouka of the Cherokees until his death in battle in 1739. His town became a center of Carolina trade and influence with Ludovic Grant as trader and promoter of Carolina interests.

In the west, with the reopening of the Creek trade in 1718, the Carolinians revived their trade with the Chickasaws who had been faithful to the English throughout the Yamasee war. While the English trade had been interrupted, French traders had gained a slight foothold. But when the English traders returned, the French found competition difficult. In 1722 the Chickasaws, emboldened by English goods and weapons, broke with the French, only to have the French send the Choctaws against them. The intensity of this war threatened the existence of the Chickasaws, and many talked of leaving their country. Carolina induced some of them to remove to the New Windsor area on Savannah River to take the place of the Shawnees who for the most part between 1700 and 1715 had migrated to Pennsylvania.

Fortunately for the Chickasaws, a faction of Choctaws, unhappy with the French trade, sought peace in order to get an English trade. Promoted by Carolina traders, a conspiracy against the French developed among the Choctaws, Chickasaws, and Natchez. The Natchez, dwelling on the Mississippi, had an oppressive French colony among them. In 1729, having been guaranteed some Choctaw and all Chickasaw support, they revolted and slaughtered most of the French. When swift and ruthless French retaliation followed, the Choctaws backed away from the affair, and those Natchez who survived the French onslaught fled to the Chickasaws. The Chickasaws, befriending the Natchez, now became engaged in a bitter war with the French which lasted for years.

Meanwhile in the Cherokee country Carolina affairs suffered a set back. Discontent with their sharp dealing traders led many Cherokees to violate Carolina law which limited their trade to their towns, by going down to Savanno town or by dealing with settlers who carried on a surreptitious trade. Carolina attempts to enforce her laws increased Cherokee unrest. Several times in 1733 Cherokees attempting to approach Charleston to trade were turned back. The frustrated Indians behaved insolently toward the back settlers and some talked with the Catawbas of killing all the traders and starting a war with the English. The Catawbas, refusing to join, reported the conspiracy to Charleston. Carolina organized a frontier patrol and sent Colonal Tobias Fitch to smooth over the troubles with the Cherokees. But early in 1734 Cherokees in the Middle Settlements plundered and wrecked a trader's store. Bad talk swelled, a trader was murdered, and many traders fled. Though rumors held that rival traders had fomented the troubles, the Cherokees had

a grievance in the higher prices traders charged to recoup
their losses from periods of cut-throat rivalry.

Carolina at once embargoed the Cherokee trade and ordered all traders who had not fled to leave. She asked Virginia to refrain from any trade with the Cherokees and
warned the Catawba traders to keep hands off. The assembly
decided not to reopen the trade until Cherokees sent deputies to promise indemnity and to agree to a Carolina fort in
the Cherokee country. In Charleston in November a dozen
important Cherokee headmen agreed to collect deerskins of
£500 value to pay for the damage and to cede Carolina a
small tract near Toogaloo for a fort. This was the first
Cherokee land cession, but Carolina did not use it. It seemed
advisable to reopen the trade before the fort could be built,
and subsequent Cherokee good behavior made a fort un-
necessary.

With the elimination of the Yamasee the Carolina trade
with the Creeks prospered. When Brims died sometime between 1730 and 1733 and his brother Chigelley succeeded
him as "Emperor," English prestige was high. Yet dis-
orders developed. Creek adventurers attacked Cherokees and
Yuchis near the Pallachicola garrison on Savannah River.
When in 1733 two traders were killed in the Creek country,
Carolina demanded satisfaction and the right to build a fort
near French Fort Toulouse. These were granted, but the fort
was not built.

The founding of Georgia in 1733 complicated Carolina-
Creek relations. Georgia claimed the Creek country and
animated by prohibitionist sentiments as well as economic
considerations set out to monopolize the Creek trade and
draw it to Savannah. Georgia ruled that all traders to In-

dians within the Georgia claim must take out Georgia
licences. In 1735 she sent an agent to the Creeks to oust or
seize all Carolina-licensed traders. She even claimed the
Cherokee country and in 1736 undertook a similar operation
there. The moves not only upset the Creeks and Cherokees
whose trade was interrupted, but also the Charleston merchants. Hobohatchey, the Upper Creek headman, went down
to Charleston where he declared that the Georgia settlement
violated the Creek-Carolina understanding of 1717 prohibit-
ing settlements south and west of the Savannah River and
that the Upper Creeks would deal only with Carolina. In the
Indian country Creeks threatened Georgia agents and protected their Carolina traders. Carolina appealed to the
Crown, which in 1737 declared the western trade open to
both Carolina and Georgia licensed traders. The two colonies
made an agreement allotting much of the Lower Creek trade
to Georgia and most of the Upper Creek trade to Carolina.
Extensive overlapping occurred, and, interestingly, Charleston merchants financed Savannah merchants. In 1736 Georgia
established Augusta as a trade base, not far from Carolina's
Fort Moore. Since the Creeks objected to the building of an
English fort in the Upper Creek country, the two colonies
cooperated in establishing a semi-fortified "warehouse"
there. The trade of both colonies prospered.

Far out toward the Mississippi Carolina goods, guns, and
ammunition maintained the Chickasaws against the French-
allied Choctaws, Arkansas, and Illinois. Supplies reached the
Chickasaws on pack horses from Augusta by the trading
path through the Lower and Upper Creeks, much to the dis-
tress of the French who attempted to bribe the Creeks into
cutting the line of communication. Through the Upper

Creek Abeikas, the English intrigued with talk of trade to detach the Choctaws from the French and secure peace for the Chickasaws. In the maze of intrigue and counter intrigue several truces occurred, but the Chickasaws persisted in attacking French convoys on the Mississippi. In 1736 Bienville planned a joint attack of French troops and Indians from Mobile and the Illinois country to exterminate the Chickasaws. Early in May the Illinois group under d'Artaguette struck the town of Chocalusa. Forewarned, the Chickasaws with the help of Carolina and Georgia traders had built blockhouses protected by earthen embankments. The French bravely attempted to storm them but were mowed down by heavy fire from traders and Chickasaws. Although the French retreated, the Chickasaws overtook and captured them. Bienville arrived two weeks later and was defeated near the Chickasaw town of Ackia. Thereafter Chickasaws and Cherokees under Carolina influence warred on the Choctaws and the Wabash River and Illinois Indians. French convoys on the Mississippi were less safe than before. But keeping the trade open to the Chickasaws was so difficult that in 1737 Carolina invited the Chickasaws to remove to join the old Chickasaw settlement at New Windsor. A small band accepted, others settled in the northern Creek country to be nearer the Creek traders, but the bulk of the Chickasaws held their old country, and Carolina and Georgia traders continued to reside among them. Intermittently in periods of truce these and their countrymen in the Abeika town traded with the Choctaws hoping to wean them from the French and bring them firmly into the Carolina trading empire. In 1738 there was a possibility of a Creek-Chickasaw-Choctaw alliance based on the English trade. Hobohatchey of Abeika brought envoys of all the nations to Charleston to seal a peace and alliance. The venture collapsed when the French at Fort Toulouse exploited divisions in the Upper Creeks.

While Carolina promoted the Cherokee alliance with the Chickasaws in raids on the Mississippi and north of the Ohio, she feared the French might draw the Cherokees away from her. In 1737 the Fort Toulouse French succeeded by way of the Creeks in bringing a Cherokee delegation to talk neutrality in the Chickasaw war. The French could not mount a trade to the Cherokee country and nothing came of it.

A much more specific worry to Carolina was the activity of Christian Priber, a German visionary, who mysteriously arrived in the Cherokee country and settled down at Great Tellico. Suspected in Carolina of being a French agent, he talked to the Indians of founding an ideal socialist community near the Creek country to which he urged the Cherokees to move. He talked against English land grabbing and urged trade with both the French and English. His talk fueled anti-English sentiment, and he became a great favorite. Carolina sent an agent to seize him, but the Indians protected him and menaced the agent. In 1738 to counter Priber and the French, Carolina invited Emperor Moytoy of Great Tellico down to Charleston. To impress him they staged an elaborate reception. A company of uniformed gentlemen on horseback escorted Moytoy into town where he watched a great parade of colony troops before the council house. With ornate speeches the governor lavished presents on the visitors and acknowledged Moytoy as "Emperor" of all the Cherokees. Moytoy responded with equal oratorical

prowess and promised undying friendship to the English—
but he refused to surrender Priber. Priber shortly left Great
Tellico for the Creek country where early in 1739 he was
seized and sent down to Savannah where he died in prison.
He seems not to have been a French agent, but a brilliant
half-mad idealist, hoping to establish a perfect society in the
American wilderness.

ountry under the direction of Eleazer Wiggan.
ad struggled with an inadequate store of goods
e Virginia Trading Company and had given up.
Virginia company went out of business in 1718,
nanaged the Catawba trade from the Congaree fort
18. With the demise of the Carolina colony trading
in 1720, private traders took over in the Catawba
nd thereafter the Catawbas looked to Charleston
on. Disease and rum took their toll. Faced with
numbers, they accepted Carolina's suggestion that
 into their tribe the remnants of the Cheraws,
Congarees, Santees, and Winyahs. Generally they
l peace with the Cherokees, who, however, were
Carolina's interest in them. Under frequent attack
Iroquois, the Catawbas had rejected repeated
invitations to fight the Creeks. Though involved
nal individual fracases with the advancing settlers,
e to settle matters in conference at Charleston.
–1745 they assisted Carolina against the Spaniards,
urn between 1740 and 1743 Carolina tried to ar-
ace for them with the Iroquois. This peace, how-
ot last. The Cherokee peace with the Iroquois had
 the flank of the Catawbas to Iroquois raids. Late
e Savannah River Chickasaws became belligerent
 Catawbas who had rejected a Creek proposal for
iglish rising. The Catawbas informed Charleston
thern Indian coalition might strike them and ap-
 help.

t he had a dangerous situation on the frontier. He
rts of Frenchmen from the Detroit-Illinois area
hota and of Shawnees talking an anti-English Indian

IV

The Creek-Cherokee War

In 1739 England went to war with Spain. Carolina and Georgia immediately set about enlisting Indian allies. They succeeded in rallying 800 Cherokees and Lower Creeks against the Spaniards in Oglethorpe's unsuccessful 1740 siege of St. Augustine. The Cherokees brought smallpox home from this expedition, and thousands of them died in the worst disaster the nation had encountered. The French, sympathetic to the Spaniards, intrigued to halt the flow of Indian allies to the English and in so doing brought on a war between the Creeks and the Cherokees. The immediate occasion for the war was the Cherokee assistance to the Chickasaws in their war against the Choctaws. The French maneuvered the Creeks into a difficult position with the Choctaws from which they could only escape by killing Cherokees who passed through their country to attack Choctaws. As the French had hoped, the Creek-Cherokee war that ensued prevented the Cherokees from sending further help to the English.

The Creek war and the smallpox havoc caused a great contraction of the Cherokee nation. They practically abandoned the upper area of Georgia on the Chatuga, Toogaloo, and Chattahoochee rivers. The Keowee River group now became the principal body of Lower Cherokees, and Skiagunsta of Keowee, recognized by Georgia as "King of the Cherokees," became an influential voice. With Skiagunsta strongly pro-Georgia, Carolina concentrated her attention on Emperor Moytoy of Great Tellico.

In the general situation Carolina could not tolerate a Creek-Cherokee war and in 1742 Lieutenant Governor William Bull arranged a peace. He then tried to counter the now dominant French influence over the Upper Creeks by sending Captain Wood there to obtain permission to build an English fort. Tempted by English presents, Creek headmen visited Charleston and agreed, but vigorous French intrigue finally induced the Upper Creeks to revert to a neutral position and oppose the fort. Meanwhile the parsimonious Carolina assembly refused to appropriate money for the fort.

By the time James Glen became governor in 1744, England was at war with France. Glen tried to use the Creeks against the French, but Creek neutralism prevailed and the effort failed. Shortly Glen was confronted by a new Creek-Cherokee war and French efforts to win over the Cherokees. These activities had resulted from a peace Lieutenant Governor Bull had arranged through the mediation of Lieutenant Governor George Clarke of New York between the Cherokees and the northern Indians. Pro-French Shawnees and Senecas from the Upper Ohio Valley now came into the Cherokee towns and not only spread anti-English talk but induced young Cherokees to go with them on raids against the Creeks. The resentful Creeks went to war against the Cherokees.

In April 1745 to counter rising pro-French sentiment among the Cherokees, Governor Glen invited Moytoy's son and successor Ammonscossittee, the young Emperor of Great Tellico, his guardian the Raven of Hiwassee, and Skiagunsta

of Keowee to Charleston fo[r]
meeting. They were entert[
dinner aboard a warship,
mansion. In ceremonial me[
Ammonscossittee dutifully
crown of the Cherokees at
to King George II. He prom[
to the northern Indians so
Creeks. Glen unctuously
prices.

But the Overhill leaders
seat of Cherokee headship,
Emperor's promises. They s[
and in the winter of 1745–17[
The Overhill conduct aros[
Carolina as from a desire
French trade with which
and lower the price of trade

But Glen conceived of
security of Carolina. In th[
by way of the Catawbas
anti-English conspiracy had
Cherokee country. Certainl[
sentiment had come into t[
Creeks, though at war with
get the word through to t[

In the spring of 1746 the
Since the Yamasee war Car[
as the bastion against incu[
northern Indians. In 1716
peace with Virginia, Caroli[

Catawba
Wiggan
against t[
When th[
Carolina
built in [
operation[
country,
for direc[
dwindlin[
they bri[
Waterees
maintain
jealous o[
from th[
Cherokee
in occasi[
they cho[
From 17[
and in r[
range a [
ever, did
opened [
in 1745 [
toward t[
an anti-[
that a sc[
pealed f[

Glen f[
had rep[
visiting [

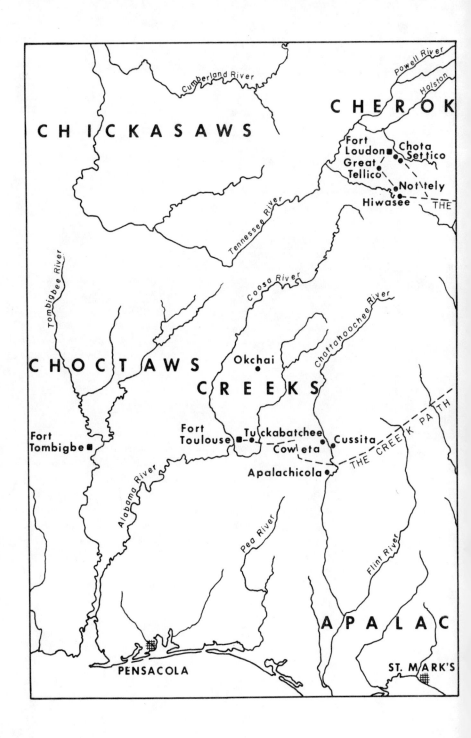

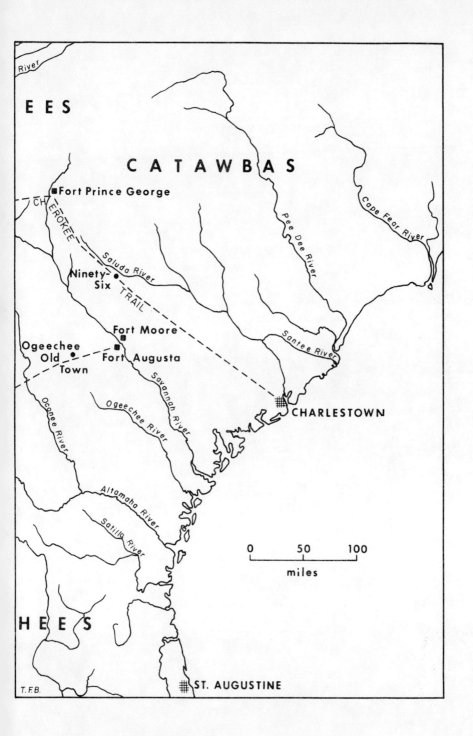

EES

CATAWBAS

River

Cape Fear River

Pee Dee River

Fort Prince George

CHEROKEE

Saluda River

Ninety-Six

TRAIL

Santee River

Fort Moore

Ogeechee Old Town

Fort Augusta

Oconee River

Ogeechee River

Savannah River

CHARLESTOWN

Altamaha River

Satilla River

0   50   100
miles

HEES

ST. AUGUSTINE

T.F.B.

coalition to the Creeks. Lower Creeks, indignant that the Florida border war with the Spaniards had become quiescent and that the English forces in Georgia had ceased bribing them to peace and neutrality, had threatened Fort Moore.

Northern Indians annoyed the frontier settlers by stealing their cattle and sometimes plundering their homes and attacked the Catawbas. Chigelley at Coweta, engaged in a land dispute with Georgia, listened to Mary Bosomworth, his half-breed relative whose claims to lands under Indian title irked Georgia.* He also listened to the French at Fort Toulouse who said that the English would eventually take all the Indian country. Everywhere there was unrest over the rising wartime prices of trade goods. In this complex situation the Chickasaw assault on the Catawbas looked to Glen like a French conspiracy. He decided upon a show of force along the frontiers with conferences with the Catawbas, Cherokees, and Creeks. With fifty mounted gentlemen and 200 colony troops he sallied forth followed by a wagon train of presents.

* Mary Bosomworth, born Coosaponokeesa, was the daughter of a sister of "Emperor" Brims of Coweta. Reputed to be the daughter of Henry Woodward, she was educated as a Christian at Pon Pon in Carolina. In the peace following the Yamasee war she was married to John Musgrove, the half-breed son of Colonel John Musgrove. She and Johnny set up in trade at Yamacraw Bluff, the site of later Savannah, where they were given lands by the Yamacraw Indians. They prospered, but after the founding of Savannah Johnny died and one of Johnny's indentured servants, Jacob Matthews, married Mary, and continued the trade. When Matthews died, Mary was one of the most prosperous people in the Savannah neighborhood with claims as an Indian to large areas of land. The adventuring English vicar, Thomas Bosomworth, married her and proceeded to lay claim to all Mary's land claims. Since these had not been granted by the colony or by the Crown, the colony objected. Bosomworth declared Mary Queen of all the Creeks by descent and entitled to whatever lands the tribe allotted her. A prolonged and bitter quarrel ensued between the Bosomworths and the colony.

In early May at the Congarees, he promised the Catawbas that he would ask the Chickasaws and Cherokees to keep the peace and handed out presents. At Ninety-Six he met the Raven of Hiwassee, Ammonscossittee, and Skiagunsta of Keowee. This band of English friends promised to remain loyal, to seize Frenchmen visiting Tanase, and to prevent northern Indians from attacking the Catawbas. At New Windsor he met Chigelley who explained away the Creek belligerence at Fort Moore. After complaining of trade prices, Chigelley agreed to treat with the British in Georgia. Having received abundant presents, he went home in an amicable frame of mind.

Glen's expansive and expensive expedition accomplished little. The Raven of Hiwassee and his pro-English faction could not induce the Overhill Cherokees to break off inter-course with the French and northern Indians who came in increasing numbers, promoted insolence toward the traders, annoyed the Catawbas, and fanned the Creek-Cherokee antipathy to new heights. Among the Lower Creeks anti-English sentiment emerged once again, animated by the Georgia-Bosomworth dispute.

Glen once again attempted to allay Creek suspicions. In October 1746 at Charleston he won a faction of the Upper Creeks under the Wolf of Muccolossus to consent to a fort in their country and to attack Fort Toulouse. But he made the mistake of angering Malatchi, Chigelley's nephew, who was about to become head of the Lower Creeks. When Malatchi opposed a fort in the Upper Creeks, Glen threatened him with a trade embargo. Malatchi went home and recommenced talks with the French. In the Upper Creeks the elders quashed talk of an English fort and attacking the

French. Only when Mary Bosomworth, having won the support of Colonel Horton, commander of the British in Georgia, sent her brother-in-law with presents to Malatchi did the Creeks simmer down.

Though Glen's diplomacy failed with the Creeks, it succeeded with the Choctaws. For a number of years Red Shoes, headman of the Eastern Choctaws, had in intervals of peace done business with the Carolina Chickasaw traders, John Campbell and James Adair. By late 1744, he had informed Lachlan McGillivray, trader among the Abeikas, that for an English trade he would desert the French. McGillivray communicated this news to Glen with a proposal that he be given a monopoly of the Choctaw trade, and in 1745 the Carolina assembly voted to do so. Glen, however, stepped into the situation with an independent company which included his brother and was later satirically styled "The Sphynx Company" because of the mystery surrounding its affairs. In the winter of 1745–1746 Glen through Adair and Campbell intrigued with Red Shoes. The traders advanced quantities of their own goods for the enterprise. Red Shoes started a war against the French. In April 1747, he sent his brother to Charleston to make an alliance and Glen sent back a convoy of ammunition and goods. But Red Shoes' effort to obtain Creek help foundered on Creek fear that an English trade to the Choctaws would make the Choctaws a more difficult future enemy. Creeks obstructed Glen's convoy to the Choctaws which suffered heavy losses of goods. Though Red Shoes effectively raided the French gulf settlements, the French in 1748 took advantage of Choctaw division and raised up a civil war among them. Lacking needed support from Carolina, Red Shoes was killed by his countrymen. By the end of

1749 the Choctaws had returned to their French alliance. The Sphynx Company went bankrupt. When Adair and Campbell petitioned the Carolina assembly for reimbursement, a violent debate erupted and Charleston was treated to a pamphlet war. Adair and Campbell, accused of falsifying their roles, were not reimbursed.

Meanwhile the Creek-Cherokee war flamed with both sides bitter against Carolina for providing ammunition to the enemy. Glen, having trouble with the Cherokees, tried to use a promise of a Creek peace to bring the Cherokees into line. In the autumn of 1746 Glen had sent George Pawley to purchase from the Lower Cherokees lands along Long Canes Creek and to Tanase to protest the presence of Frenchmen. Old Hop of Chota, now great ouka of the Cherokees, and his council, angry at Glen's favors to the Hiwassee and Tellico people, permitted northern Indians at Tanase to beat up Pawley's party. The Tanase-Chota towns then told Pawley that if Carolina wished favors from them, she should shift her attentions from the Raven of Hiwassee and Amonscossittee to them. They said that if they were to give up their friendship with the northern Indians, Glen must build them a fort. Glen angrily demanded compensation for the assault on Pawley and that the Overhills immediately forbid the northern Indians hospitality. Since a break with the northerners was unthinkable in the midst of the Creek war, Chota-Tanase refused.

In 1748 Shawnees from the Logstown area, visiting the Cherokees, seized the Carolina surveyors, George Haig and William Brown, and carried them off to the Ohio. On the way Haig was killed. In the Cherokee Lower Towns, the head warrior Wawhatchee, upset by high trade prices and friendly to the Shawnees, talked of killing all the traders. Outraged by these events, Glen embargoed the Cherokee trade and called the headmen to Charleston. The Tanase-Chotas ducked the meeting. The Hiwassee-Tellicos attended, and, as usual, agreed to all Glen's demands including giving up Wawhatchee to be punished. They promised to attack the northern Indians and break Tanase-Chota's peace with them. Glen agreed to reopen the trade and to mediate peace with the Creeks. As a result in September 1749 Creek deputies met the Raven of Hiwassee and Ammonscossittee at Charleston and made peace. Both sides agreed that Carolina should embargo trade with whichever party renewed hostilities. By this time the French-English war had ended, and Glen had called off the Hiwassee-Tellico war against the French northern Indians.

The Creek-Cherokee peace of 1749 failed. French inspired rumors that Cherokees and northern Indians had attacked Creek hunting parties set off new Creek attacks on the Cherokees. Glen, holding the Creeks responsible, threatened an embargo. Thereupon the Gun Merchant of Okchai, an Upper Creek headman, hastened to make peace with the Cherokees. But Malatchi of the Lower Creeks refused to make peace until the Cherokees drove out all northern Indians. When he informed the French that they would be welcome in his country, Glen, fearing French influence, decided not to embargo the Creek trade.

Early in 1751 northern Indians entered the Cherokee country and urged the Cherokees to loot their traders. Finally Lower Cherokees, along with northerners pursuing a Creek war party, killed a trader. Glen embargoed the Cherokee trade and demanded satisfaction. War talk filled the Chero-

kee towns, but, denied ammunition, the Cherokees were at
the mercy of the Creeks and English. Therefore, in November the Raven of Hiwassee and Skiagunsta of Keowee went to
Charleston. They agreed to surrender the murderers of the
trader, to pay for looted goods, and, as before, to bar the
northern Indians. Glen promised to lift the embargo, to
build a fort at Skiagunsta's town of Keowee to discourage
the northern Indians, and to make a peace with the Creeks.

Glen's attempt at a Creek peace failed. The Carolina assembly refused to vote money for the Keowee fort, and the
northern Indians came as usual. At Coweta Malatchi kept
his warriors out against the Cherokees.

However, in April 1752 Glen was forced to act. Acorn
Whistler, a Creek warrior, had driven a Cherokee hunting
party down country, following them until they sought protection in Charleston. The Whistler then boldly entered Charleston where the authorities apprehended him and exacted a
promise not to molest the Cherokees. Released, he laid an
ambush outside the town and killed the Cherokees as they
set out for home under his promise of their safety. Whistler
then fled to the Creek country where he proudly displayed
the Cherokees' scalps. Cherokee leaders accused Carolina of
complicity and made threats. Glen then decided he must
force the Creeks to make peace and to punish the Whistler.
Since Mary Bosomworth and her English husband Thomas
were in Charleston at the time, Glen decided to use Mary's
influence to effect his ends. She and Thomas carried to
Malatchi at Coweta Glen's threats of embargo unless Whistler
were punished. Malatchi, knowing that he could not get the
Creeks publicly to punish the Whistler, maneuvered pri-
vately to have him assassinated by one of his relatives who

alleged that the Whistler had meddled with his wife. The
Coweta headman then agreed to peace with the Cherokees.
These arrangements took more than a year. Malatchi made
it clear that the northerners, particularly the Senecas of the
New York Six Nations must give up their southern incursions.
This Glen effected through Governor George Clinton of
New York. To further the work of peace Glen was forced
to give up his reliance upon the Raven of Hiwassee and
Ammonscossittee of Tellico and to treat with Chota-Tanase
as the rightful leadership of the Cherokees. This change
came from the shrewd diplomacy of the Overhill Second
Man, Attakullaculla, or the Little Carpenter, who, bent on
obtaining lower prices in the trade, refused to make peace
with the Creeks, and threatened to bring in Virginia traders unless prices were lowered. Glen complied and also
recognized Old Hop of Chota as rightful "Emperor of the
Cherokees."

Alarmed by Overhill power, Glen decided to raise up
Lower Cherokee power by building his fort at Keowee and
in October 1753 erected Fort Prince George. Old Hop and
Malatchi finally concluded a Creek-Cherokee peace that
lasted.

An objective in the establishment of Fort Prince George
was to prevent the northern Indians from basing on the
Lower Cherokee towns for attacks on the Catawbas and
forays against the horses and cattle of settlers. Most of the
raids were made by Upper Ohio River Shawnees and Senecas
and the Canadian Caughnawagas. Although the Catawbas
had fought fiercely, their numbers dwindled. They needed
peace for survival but were too proud to beg for it. In 1751
Glen through Governor Clinton of New York arranged a

peace meeting of Catawba King Haigler and Iroquois at
Albany. But the French in Canada deeming it necessary for
the safety of Canada to keep Canadian Indians engaged in
far away adventures did not want peace in the south. War
there they knew weakened Carolina's defences; therefore,
they kept the Caughnawagas stirred up to attack, and Six
Nations Iroquois for adventure and glory joined in. By 1754
the Catawbas were desperate. They had but 200 warriors.
Their repeated land sales to South Carolinians and the ad-
vance of North Carolina settlers had much reduced their
hunting grounds to the south and east. To protect them, for
they were not only a bastion but also available to put down
possible slave revolts, Glen early in 1755 in conference with
King Haigler at Charleston agreed to prohibit settlement
within thirty miles of their country. Negotiations with North
Carolina were unsuccessful, and North Carolinians moved
to within six miles of the Catawba country. Yet so devoted
to the English were the Catawbas that they served effectively
with the Virginian and British forces throughout the French
and Indian war.

V

Carolina's Cherokee War

The rivalry of France and England for possession of the interior of North America which culminated in the French and Indian War (1755–1763) plunged Carolina more deeply into Cherokee and Creek affairs. Glen sought to enlist both tribes as allies. The Creeks did not succumb. For a while in 1755 it seemed he had scored a triumph when at Charleston in conference with the Gun Merchant he obtained permission to build a fort in the Upper Creek country in return for concessions in trade practices and prices. But tribal councils repudiated the Gun Merchant's treaty. Torn by quarrels between pro-French and pro-English factions and warned by Cherokees not to tolerate an English establishment deep in their country, they elected traditional neutrality.

Glen was more successful with the Cherokees. Spurred by his ambition to make an imperial record and by fears for the Carolina trade monopoly, he labored to thwart both Virginia and French threats. Late in 1753 Governor Robert Dinwiddie of Virginia, planning to retake the Forks of the Ohio from the French who had ousted the Virginians from a post they were building there, sent to Chota for Cherokee help. Chota suggested that Virginia open a trade with the Overhills. To block this threat to Carolina trade, Glen informed the Overhills that Dinwiddie did not need their

help, and he informed Dinwiddie that overtures to the Cherokees must be made through Carolina lest inter-colonial
rivalry alienate the Cherokees from the English. Dinwiddie
had already sent an agent to the Overhills with a promise of
a trade if they sent deputies to talk with him.

Meanwhile Chota had entertained French Indians from
Detroit who won over the Little Carpenter and Old Hop
with an offer of a French trade. Thereupon the Carolina
traders pressured their friends and debtors to beat up the
Little Carpenter. The Little Carpenter then decided the best
interests of the Cherokees lay with the English and the
Carolina trade. He induced the Great Warrior Oconostota to
go out against the French allied Choctaws, and he himself
led a war party against French convoys on the Mississippi.
In private talks with Virginia agents he said Glen had
blocked help to Virginia but that if Virginia could produce
a sizeable trade, he and Old Hop might be interested in help-
ing Virginia sometime in the future. No Cherokees aided the
ill-fated Virginia 1754 expedition under George Washington.

In the summer of 1754 northern Indians retaliated for
Little Carpenter's spring raids. They caused havoc in the
Middle Settlements and the Cherokees thought better of
neutrality. Old Hop sent to Glen for guns and ammunition,
blaming Carolina for the attacks. Glen deemed the situation
ripe for launching his boldest project, that of inducing the
Cherokees to cede all their lands to the English crown
and of permitting the English to build a fort among the
Overhills by which he could clinch the territories and trade
for Carolina. He demanded that before he sent help, the
Cherokees must send deputies to Charleston.

Old Hop had second thoughts. Not wishing to alienate

Carolina, he sent to Glen acknowledging English sovereignty over Cherokee lands, but he refused to send deputies. He listened to Creeks prophesying that English forts in Indian country would lead to the enslavement of the Indians and to his own people who complained of trader pressure to pay their debts. He opened correspondence with Governor Louis de Kerlerec of Louisiana.

In the midst of this unrest, Dinwiddie, now hoping for Cherokee auxiliaries to accompany Braddock's 1755 expedition against the forks of the Ohio, sent an agent to the Overhills with a promise of "a great and constant trade." Interested, Old Hop and the Little Carpenter promised help. With this prospect of breaking the Carolina monopoly, they informed Glen that deputies would come to talk about a fort. Glen by this time had learned from Dinwiddie that the Crown had allotted £1,000 for the Carolina fort, and he determined to get the Cherokees down before they flocked to support Braddock.

The Cherokees did not join Braddock. After Braddock's disaster, Dinwiddie blamed Glen. But other forces had restrained the Cherokees. Hardly had Old Hop and the Little Carpenter agreed to help Braddock, than Shawnees from French Fort Duquesne, Braddock's objective, came into Chota to advise the Cherokees to remain neutral. Shortly thereafter northern Indians killed some Cherokees and blocked the road to Virginia. The Overhills decided to be neutral and cancelled all war parties intended for the Braddock campaign. The Little Carpenter and his deputies hesitated to go to Charleston. Late in April he informed Glen that the headmen feared to go far from the nation, that Glen must come halfway to meet them. Glen raised up all the colony gentlemen as

cavalry and with 500 militiamen and a long wagon train of
presents went up to Saluda. There he met 500 Cherokees led
by Old Hop and the Little Carpenter. With extensive oratory
the two Cherokee headmen ceded to the Crown "all the lands
on each side of the Tennessee as far as the Mississippi and
all from the Tennessee to the Ohio River." Glen promised
to improve trade and to build a fort among the Overhills to
protect them from the French and their Indians. The fort
would also protect Carolina trade from Virginian interlopers
and would strengthen the Little Carpenter's generally pro-
Carolina position.

But Glen could not build the fort. His assembly refused
to supplement the insufficient Crown grant until he would
agree to the Crown's reimbursing the assembly. A long legis-
lative battle ensued. The Little Carpenter, his prestige falling
among his people, came to Charleston to urge haste, but to
no avail. Not until May 1756 did Glen yield to his assembly.
He then started out with a force to build the fort, only to
learn on the road that William Henry Lyttelton had arrived
in Charleston to supplant him as governor. He sent part of
his force to Fort Prince George to await the new governor's
instructions and returned to Charleston.

In March Dinwiddie sent commissioners to meet the Cherokees at Broad River with promises to help build Carolina's
fort and to open a trade at once in return for warriors to
defend the Virginia frontier. Before the Virginians could
arrive, pro-French Cherokees, angry at rising wartime prices
and backed by the Mortar, a pro-French Creek, demanded
that negotiations be opened with the French. Delay was
causing the English position to crumble. Virginia forces
arrived at Chota in June and found no Carolina fort builders

there. The Little Carpenter forced them to build a small fort, but since they had no orders to garrison it, it only increased Overhill anger with the English. Old Hop pursued a pro-French policy and no warriors went to Virginia.

In Charleston, Lyttelton, having Crown orders to cooperate with Virginia, labored to get the assembly to rescind their limitations upon any grant for the fort. Aware of the Overhill unrest, he turned to the Lower Cherokees under Wawhatchee who were jealous of the attention the Overhills had received and urged them to visit him for presents. They came willingly and were so bedazzled with parades and presents that they repudiated Chota leadership and promised to send warriors to Virginia. The assembly finally made an unconditional grant for the Overhill fort, and Lyttelton dispatched forces under Captains Raymond Demere and John Stuart to build elaborate Fort Loudoun near Chota. Chota overawed by the presence of 300 English and colony troops subsided into a show of friendship. The Little Carpenter's prestige rose and became ascendant when Old Hop's missions to New Orleans and Detroit returned with word that the French could not support a Cherokee trade. Because of wartime delays and shortages no trade came from Virginia, so the Overhills remained tied to Carolina, yet they still sent no warriors to Virginia. The Lower Towns, however, remained true to their commitments and sent large numbers of warriors to Virginia in 1757.

In the Creek country Lyttelton made no more progress than had Glen. He hoped the Gun Merchant would eventually obtain ratification of the fort treaty. Aware that the Mortar, who opposed the fort, allied Creek nativism with Cherokee unrest, he sent Captain Dan Pepper to the Upper Creeks to

strengthen the pro-English faction and push ratification of
the fort treaty. Pepper was well received by both Lower and
Upper Creeks, but, though supported by the pro-English Wolf
of Muccolossus, he could not upset the forces which sustained
neutrality. Glen's policy of imperial expansion in the Creek
country died on Lyttelton's hands.

In the light of events in the Cherokee and Creek nations,
it appears that Charleston's economic interests exaggerated
the Mortar's influence and the French threat in order to
induce the home government to send a British garrison to
Charleston. The gold which this garrison must pay for its
subsistence would enhance the Carolina economy. A bat-
talion of troops came, and Charleston flourished. All during
1757 Lyttelton had a peaceful and prosperous Indian frontier, and settlers moved westward toward Ninety-Six and
into the Long Canes country which the Cherokees had ceded
in 1746. When, that autumn, Lyttelton ordered the giving of
presents and ammunition at Fort Loudoun to those Cherokees who would go to Virginia's aid, Overhill warriors
flocked north.

In 1758 the frontier peace began to disintegrate. The Long
Canes settlers angered the Lower Cherokees by invading
their hunting grounds. When in the winter of 1757–1758 a
Cherokee hunting party toward Edisto River was robbed
and murdered, they suspected the whites and talked war.
Lyttelton attempted to smooth over the incident as the
work of enemy Indians. Truculent Cherokees, going north
under Seroweh of Estatoe secretly murdered two North
Carolinians and took their scalps which Seroweh tried to
palm off on Virginia authorities as French for the reward
Virginia offered. Betrayed by some of his own, Seroweh was

rebuffed at Winchester by Colonel George Washington and,
disgruntled, set out for home stealing horses on the way.
The Virginia frontiersmen were angry. Seroweh's activity
resulted in a series of armed clashes in which Virginians and
Cherokees from Estatoe were killed.

When in late May reports of these events reached the
Cherokee nation, war talk swelled. Old Hop and the Little
Carpenter, aware that the Cherokees would suffer if they lost
their English trade, forbade all war preparations. Lyttelton
also dampened war ardor by threatening to attack unless the
Cherokees made reparation for Virginians killed and horses
stolen. The Little Carpenter set out for Virginia to join the
British forces and to attempt to smooth over matters with
the Virginia government. While he was on his way a new
clash occurred, provoked by scalp-hunting Virginians seeking
to collect from Cherokee heads Virginia bounties for enemy
scalps. After one Cherokee escaped to tell the story, Cherokee
parties itching for revenge set out for Virginia. Lyttelton
sent to the nations promises of satisfaction to the relatives
of slain Cherokees upon recall of the war parties. If the
Cherokees would not accept this solution, he would embargo
the trade. The Cherokees yielded, recalled the warriors, and
the offended relatives went to Charleston to accept presents.
By then the Little Carpenter, finding himself distrusted by
British General John Forbes, had gone to Williamsburg
where a lively encounter with Governor Francis Fauquier
resulted in an agreement to forget the past and a promise
of a Virginia trade at once. The Little Carpenter returned
to the Overhills in the early spring of 1759 to announce his
diplomatic triumph in breaking the Carolina trade monopoly
as the strongest reason against war. Though Lyttelton, in-

formed of General Forbes' distrust of the Cherokee leader,
summoned the Little Carpenter to Charleston and rebuked
him for deserting the British army, the Little Carpenter
promised to support all efforts to keep the peace. But Lyttelton sent Lieutenant Richard Coytmore, a tougher commander, to Fort Prince George.

Among the Overhills Towns events were slipping beyond
the Little Carpenter's grasp. The Mortar, frustrated by his
fellow Creeks in his anti-English designs, went to the Cherokee country and secretly chided relatives of Cherokees slain
in Virginia for not taking vengeance. Shamed, warriors of
Overhill Settico stole away in the spring to the North Carolina frontier and took nineteen white scalps, one for each
of their Estatoe kinsmen killed by Virginians. These they
carried boastfully into Keowee where Lieutenant Coytmore
protested strongly. The Little Carpenter, returning from
Charleston, beheld at Keowee the undoing of all his painful
diplomacy. Knowing that the Cherokees would never yield
the scalpers to the English and that they themselves could
not physically punish them, the Little Carpenter sent to Old
Hop to order Settico to surrender the scalps and have them
buried, a ceremonial rebuke. As he travelled home at all the
towns he talked against war and argued that the affair was
Settico's only, that the nation should not become involved.
At Chota, he found the Overhill Cherokees hostile to Captain
Paul Demere, who had succeeded his brother at Fort Loudoun and who demanded the surrender of the murderers.
He convinced Demere that this was impossible, and Demere,
realizing that if war came his force would be isolated, agreed
to the surrender and burial of the scalps. The Little Carpenter, to render war with the English impossible by keeping

the Cherokees at war with the French, then led a war party against the French on the Mississippi. In his absence, the Overhills, fearing that Carolina would not accept his resolution of the affair, communicated with the French at Fort Toulouse to learn whether if they were obliged to defend themselves, the French could supply them. The French could not.

Carolina did not want a frontier war. Lyttelton, on receiving the bad news from Coytmore and an apology from Keowee, awaited formal complaint from North Carolina. Meanwhile Cherokees from Estatoe took three scalps in South Carolina. Coytmore demanded the punishment of the murderers, but Wawhatchee refused and talked with visiting Creeks of rising against the English. Cherokees carried English scalps into the Creeks and demanded that the Creek anti-English faction make good on the war talk they had peddled among the Cherokees. A plan for a joint rising of nativist Creeks and Cherokees on August 24 developed.

In the Lower Creeks a few prestigious headmen shared the Mortar's animosity toward the English. Among these were Togulki of Coweta, heir of the now dead Malatchi, and his guardian Ishenpoaphe, who in July had visited the Lower Cherokees and intimated that if the Cherokees rose, the Creeks would join. They spoke for themselves, since most Creek headmen favored neutrality.

At the time Edmund Atkin, His Majesty's Superintendent of Indian Affairs in the Southern District, visited the Upper Creeks. His presence with an armed bodyguard and his success in negotiating a trade treaty with the Choctaws spoke vividly of English power. The Mortar could only put on a show of acquiescence while his schemes, promoted by Togulki and Ishenpoaphe, matured in the Cherokee country.

The plot misfired. With Cherokee war parties stealing toward the Carolina frontier, Coytmore's spies apprised him of events. Coytmore dispatched messages to Lyttelton and to Atkin. Atkin confronted the Creek headmen who denied all knowledge of the enterprise and sent a warning to the Lower Towns to avoid complicity. Perceiving the plot exposed, the conspirators could not act. Toward the English they blandly behaved as if nothing had been intended. The Cherokee war parties, recalled, sneaked home.

Meanwhile Lyttelton had declared an embargo on the Cherokees. The angered conspirators set a new date for the rising. Dissidents began shooting at frontiersmen in the woods. Pro-English Cherokees endeavored to quash war talk. Some even threatened to kill the Creek conspirators. Togulki and Ishenpoaphe left the country and went down to Fort Moore where they serenely blamed the Cherokees for all that had happened. Nevertheless, in the Overhills, Indians killed a Fort Loudoun soldier and a trader. Though it appeared that war could not be averted, caution prevailed. Oconostota knew that the French could not supply the Cherokees and that the Cherokees probably could not sustain a war. Captain Demere induced him to go down to Fort Prince George to ask that the embargo be lifted. Oconostota's arrival at Keowee on September 20 to talk peace undercut the conspirators. At Fort Prince George, Coytmore persuaded the Great Warrior to go to Charleston, knowing that while he was among the English there would be no Cherokee war. In the Upper Creek country on September 28 an attempt to assassinate Edmund Atkin miscarried.

Lyttelton determined on a show of force in the Cherokee

country. When Oconostota arrived with a sizeable following of headmen to talk peace, he told him that all the Cherokee deputies were prisoners and must accompany the army to Keowee. Early in December 1759 Lyttelton at the head of 1,200 militia reached Fort Prince George, but nobody would treat with him, since the Cherokees were wild at his holding their peace envoys. The Little Carpenter, who had returned from his anti-French raid, after vainly trying to induce Old Hop to treat, boldly took the responsibility upon himself and went down to see Lyttelton. Under the guns of fort and army he made a treaty, whereby, in return for reopening the trade and freeing the captive deputies, the Cherokees would deliver up those Indians who had murdered white men. Though the deputies were to be ransomed one by one as the guilty were delivered, he effected the immediate release of Oconostota and three others. Lyttelton, his army disintegrating under a smallpox scare and the approaching expiration of enlistments, returned to Charleston, leaving twenty Cherokee headmen, including Wawhatchee, prisoners in Fort Prince George to be exchanged as the Cherokees fulfilled the Little Carpenter's agreement.

The enraged Indians, however, would not surrender any of the murderers. They determined on war, and the traders, who had remained in the hopes of peace, began to run. On January 19 Seroweh attempted to enter Fort Prince George to release the prisoners, but Coytmore managed to slam the gates against him. Indian warriors surged out against the Carolina frontier, and settlers fled. On February 1, a Cherokee host caught the panicking Long Canes people as they ran for Fort Moore and killed twenty-three. Other war parties hit Ninety-Six and William Miller's fort.

Among the Overhills the Little Carpenter strove for a new peace formula and to prevent the seige of Fort Loudoun. He still hoped to obtain the release of the hostages held in Fort Prince George, but he was too late. Going down to Keowee with Oconostota to negotiate, he learned that the war had begun. On February 16, secretly leaving the Little Carpenter, Oconostota lured Coytmore to the river bank for a peace conference and signaled his assassination by hidden riflemen. Inside the fort in violent retaliation the garrison massacred the hostages. The Cherokees laid siege to Fort Prince George, and fresh war parties plunged deeply into Carolina and southwestern Virginia, massacring the people and laying waste the countryside. The Carolina frontier was driven back a hundred miles.

Early in February Lyttelton learned that his peace had failed. He called on the assembly to authorize a regiment of 1,000 men for the duration of the war, asked Virginia to aid Fort Loudoun, and sent to New York for regulars to assist in an attack upon the Cherokee Lower Towns. General Jeffrey Amherst assigned 1,500 regulars under Colonel Archibald Montgomery to the expedition which assembled rapidly and began its march from Charleston on April 23. But already the Cherokees were talking peace. The Little Carpenter had halted the siege of Fort Loudoun begun by his opponents, and Cherokee efforts to enlist the Creeks had failed. Moreover at Fort Prince George, Coytmore's successor, Ensign Alexander Miln, had by stratagem, seized new Cherokee hostages including Tistoe of Keowee and Serowch. The Cherokees had no disposition to attack Montgomery's approaching army.

On the night of June 1–2, Montgomery struck. Bypassing

Fort Prince George he hit New Keowee and Estatoe. By
daylight the regulars were burning villages from which most
of the Cherokees had fled. He then encamped by Fort
Prince George and in a noble gesture ordered the release of
Miln's hostages and awaited a Cherokee bid for peace.

Nearly all the Lower Townsmen had fled to the Middle
Settlements where they were joined by Tistoe and Seroweh
who, angered by the treachery that had entrapped them,
demanded vengeance. Montgomery, receiving no peace overtures, marched for the Middle Settlements. Tistoe and Seroweh laid a trap for him on the path up the Little Tennessee
at Tessente where Montgomery's troops, rallying from surprise, made a hot fight before driving off the Cherokees.
However, having seventy wounded to care for, Montgomery
decided to retreat. Returning to Fort Prince George, he
strengthened the garrison and marched d o w n c o u n t r y.
Though they had lost forty or fifty men and had been forced
from the field, the Indians regarded the battle as a victory.
Montgomery reported his campaign a success and, after leaving a garrison at the Congarees, returned to New York.

Over the hills, the warriors had forced the Little Carpenter
to go into hiding and had begun a siege of Fort Loudoun,
which place Montgomery's retreat had doomed. Hoping for
relief from Carolina or Virginia, Demere held out until
August 7 when starvation forced him to surrender. He was
granted the right to march his troops to Fort Prince George,
but a day's march down the path they were ambushed.
Twenty-six including Demere were killed and the rest taken
prisoner.

Though they talked of taking Fort Prince George, the
Cherokees, having had their revenge, decided on opening

peace talks. Oconostota, believing he could obtain favorable terms, moved with 1,000 warriors toward Fort Prince George. On the way, he heard that a Virginia force under Colonel William Byrd was advancing toward the Overhill towns, but that Byrd would talk peace if deputies were sent to him. This turn of events had been accomplished by the Little Carpenter who had come out of hiding and gone to see Byrd. Oconostota, therefore, returned to Chota.

When word of the Fort Loudoun massacre reached Lieutenant Governor Bull, who had taken over from Lyttelton, he sent orders to Fort Prince George to accept a truce and play along with peace talks until he and General Amherst could make a decision. Over the hills peace talks dragged until the Virginians withdrew to winter quarters. Oconostota, having received encouragement from the French, went down to New Orleans where he discovered that British mastery of the seas prevented the French from supplying him. He returned in the knowledge he must make peace. But Amherst and Bull had decided differently. They dispatched a new expedition of 2,800 regulars and provincials under Colonel James Grant against the Cherokees. On June 10 near Tessente the Cherokees again attacked. They threw their weight against the two-mile-long packtrain and only desperate action by the provincials under Colonel Thomas Middleton saved the expedition. Repulsed, the Indians drew off, and Grant advanced to occupy the abandoned Middle Settlements but was unable to bring the Cherokees to a decisive action. He burned the Middle Settlements and uprooted the gardens and cornfields. Then discovering that his soldiers' footgear was worn out, he withdrew to Fort Prince George to await peace overtures.

Virginians were advancing on the Overhills Towns now crowded with Indian refugees. Oconostota sent old Caesar, the former slave, down to see Grant who assured him that unless an immediate peace was made, the British would march on the Overhills. Oconostota then sent the Little Carpenter with pipe and tobacco to hear the terms. These included the surrender of all prisoners. But the Little Carpenter perceiving the worn army gear, knew the army could not attack. He held out against the terms, and Grant sent him down to Charleston to talk. Meeting the Carolina council on September 19, 1761, the Little Carpenter induced them to drop the demand for hostages but yielded up most of the Lower Towns' hunting grounds northwest of Long Canes Creek and Ninety-Six.

Implementing the terms was difficult. Grant retired down country and the Virginians made a separate peace with the Overhills. Oconostota, refusing to meet either Virginians or Carolinians, went off to the French. The Lower Towns hedged on the Little Carpenter's land cession, and numbers of Indians refused to give up white captives. Two years passed before all the terms were fulfilled and then only after Carolina had yielded a bit to the Lower Towns on the land cession. Carolina reestablished the trade through a government monopoly. An English garrison remained at Fort Prince George. Settlers flowed over the old Lower Towns hunting grounds, and the Cherokees faced a new peril, the crunch of English land hunger. The Carolina-Cherokee trade never again reached the importance it had held before the war.

VI

Imperial Control

In 1763 management of southern Indian affairs passed from provincial to crown hands with John Stuart as Superintendent of Indian Affairs in the Southern District. The Cherokees were restive over the colony operated trading system and the uncertain boundary between the Lower Towns and the Long Canes settlement. In November 1763 at a great meeting of southern governors and the Indian tribes at Augusta, Stuart promised to settle the Cherokee boundary and return the Cherokee trade to private hands at better prices. On his request the Crown ordered Carolina to discontinue its stores and to allow private traders to reenter the Cherokee towns.

The Cherokee-South Carolina boundary was settled by the treaty of Fort Prince George, October 19, 1765. The line, surveyed in 1766, ran from ten miles west of Long Canes at Dewitt's Corner to the Savannah River and east to Reedy Creek. The survey did much to allay Cherokee unrest. Nevertheless the Carolina assembly in the spring of 1765 authorized a fort to protect the Long Canes settlers. Known as Fort Charlotte, it was built in the winter of 1765–1766.

Meanwhile the Catawbas were on the verge of extinction. They had served with the Virginians in the French and Indian war and had suffered heavy losses. In 1759 they had suffered from a smallpox epidemic. North Carolinians had encroached on their lands. By 1760 they numbered but 300, only seventy of whom were warriors. They had become largely dependent upon Carolina for gifts of food and cloth-ing to sustain them. When in 1760 Edmund Atkin, then Superintendent of the Southern Indians, heard that the Cherokees attempted to get them to fight the English, he worked out an agreement whereby, in return for a perpetual homeland, they would aid Carolina against the Cherokees. At the Augusta meeting in 1763 Stuart promised them a survey to set the boundaries of their lands. This was accom-plished in 1764, and henceforth they were wards of Carolina on a reservation fifteen miles square.

From 1766 on, the Cherokees, subjected to raids by the Iroquois and invasion of their lands by North Carolinians, were open to the intrigues of the western Indians opposing further white encroachments. Stuart and his deputy for the Cherokees, Alexander Cameron, won their confidence by arranging for a peace with the Iroquois in 1767–1768 and arranging for surveys of the North Carolina and Virginia boundaries at the treaty of Lochaber in 1768.

Frontier alarms, however, did not cease. Sparked by over-the-mountain intrigues and by very real unrest with the growing debt to the traders, the Cherokees in the winter of 1770–1771 talked war. The Carolina frontier panicked. In delicate negotiations with Oconostota, now first ouka of the Cherokees, Cameron managed to quiet war talk and the settlers returned to their homes. Shortly there developed a great Cherokee land sale scheme, whereby the Cherokees in return for forgiveness of debts would cede their land in

northeast Georgia. The deal required Crown and Creek consent and was not consummated until 1773.

Despite all treaties, land cessions, and boundary markings
whites continued to invade the Cherokee hunting grounds.
Some never returned; nevertheless Cherokee leadership assured Stuart and Cameron that no war was intended. When
in the early autumn of 1774, young Cherokees showed a
disposition to join the Shawnee war against Virginia, Cameron induced the principal headmen to assassinate the youth-
ful leaders and to restrain their warriors.

The American Revolution brought disaster to the Cherokees. In June 1775 the Carolina rebels, suspecting Stuart
of intending to use the Indians against them, forced the
Superintendent to flee to St. Augustine, leaving Cameron
in the Cherokee country to his own devices. Confusion on
the seaboard had interrupted the Cherokee trade, but the
upcountry, especially the region between Broad and Saluda
rivers, was strongly loyalist. Cameron worked to develop a
loyalist-Cherokee rapport. However, some of the traders had
strong rebel connections and talked an anti-Cameron line
to the Indians. Though confused by the conflicting points
of view, most of the Cherokees took their cues from Cameron. In the summer the provincial Committee of Safety
sent William Henry Drayton from Charleston in an attempt
to win over the loyalists and encourage the Cherokees to
neutrality. Later, the Committee, in the knowledge that the
interruption of trade caused Indian unrest, sent up a convoy
of ammunition to the Cherokees to enable them to hunt and
to prove that the rebels were not hostile. Frontier loyalists
seized the ammunition on the suspicion that the rebels intended to arm the Indians against them. The Committee,

suspecting Cameron's hand, planned to capture him, and through sympathetic traders they attempted to spirit up the Cherokees to help. Cameron fled from his home at Hard Labour to the Overhills.

From St. Augustine Stuart sought means of supplying the Cherokees with hunting ammunition from Pensacola. In September he received orders from General Thomas Gage, British Commander-in-chief in North America, to enlist the southern Indians against the rebels. Fearing that loosing the Indians on the frontier would injure loyalists as well as rebels, Stuart hesitated to carry out this order. He thought that a unilateral Indian attack without definite British invasion of the Carolina seaboard would be futile. Moreover, the rebels having seized an English ship laden with ammunition for the Indian trade and the Crown having cut off colony trade, he could not sustain the Indians in war. Eventually he was forced to act. Cherokee deputies came to him at St. Augustine, and, while asserting their loyalty, pleaded for supplies if they were to be effective British allies. Soon he learned that Sir Henry Clinton had superseded Gage and planned a southern invasion. By this time loyalist traders had removed from Charleston to Pensacola. Stuart was able to outfit a packtrain led by his brother Henry to the Cherokee country with orders to hold the Indians back until Crown forces struck Carolina.

Henry Stuart's packtrain did not arrive among the distressed Cherokees until April 1776. By then the Overhills had begun receiving Carolina loyalists fleeing rebel threats. Stuart and Cameron hoped to enlist these as guides in the proposed attacks on the frontier. Thus the offensive could be a controlled affair which would not harm loyalists. But the Cherokee young men resented controls. Inspired by Dragging Canoe they talked unrestrained war against the settlers at Watauga and on Nolichucky River.

The rebels made a strong effort to obtain Creek and Cherokee pledges to neutrality. In early May 1776, commissioners of the Continental Congress met the Creeks at Augusta and some of the Cherokees at Fort Charlotte. They peddled distrust of Stuart and Cameron and promised to reopen the trade and to remove settlers from the disputed areas. Those Cherokees who attended returned to their towns and proclaimed that they had met the commissioners only to obtain presents, which consisted mostly of rum. Nevertheless Carolina rebel traders in the Lower and Valley towns schemed to enlist an Indian following, and the British agents believed the Cherokees would go with whichever side could supply them. They sent off to Pensacola for more goods.

Overhill events pointed to a crisis when northern Indians— Shawnees, Delawares, and Senecas—acting as agents of Guy Carleton in Canada, came to talk war. They spoke in the name of all the western conspiracies of the past decade— urging war against the frontiersmen. Dragging Canoe's war faction responded favorably. When Cameron sent a warning to all loyalists at Watauga and Nolichucky to leave, the Indians suspected him of siding with the settlers. They determined to strike at once. An Indian war was coming whether or not the British attacked Charleston, and Cameron thought he should put himself at the head of it if he wished to exercise the least control. He only hoped to hold back the Indian onslaught until he had word of a successful landing by the British at Charleston.

In Carolina another move was underway to seize Cameron. Seeking him, a small rebel party under Captain McCall passed through several Lower Cherokee Towns without hindrance. On the night of June 26 it was attacked by Cherokees, five of its number killed, and McCall taken prisoner. With this bloodshed, the frontier war began. Though on June 28, the British fleet was repulsed at Charleston, on July 1 the Cherokees flooded out to war against the Carolina frontier and against Watauga and Nolichucky. With fire and massacre of rebel and loyalist alike, the Lower Cherokees swept the Carolina frontier back in horror and panic.

After the first shock the forces of retribution rallied. In a few days Major Andrew Williamson gathered several score riders and headed toward the Lower Towns. On July 15 after a sharp fight at Seneca they awaited the arrival of the Third South Carolina Provincial Regiment. In early August with 1,200 men Williamson moved forward and by the end of the month had destroyed the Cherokee Lower Towns which were abandoned on his approach. Then, joined by North Carolina forces under General Griffith Rutherford, he laid waste the Middle Settlements. In September the combined forces moved toward the Valley. On their way they fought a major battle at Wayah Gap where they barely avoided defeat in ambush. Moving ahead, they laid waste the Valley while a Virginia force led by Colonel William Christian marched on the Overhill towns.

Dragging Canoe and Cameron fled southward. Oconostota and the Little Carpenter, seeing their country again devastated and their people facing extinction, made peace. Dragging Canoe assembled warriors in the Chickamauga area of northwest Georgia from which, supplied by Stuart, he carried on a vendetta against Watauga, Nolichucky, and the Kentucky settlements. Hundreds of Cherokees had fled into the Creek towns where they spread tales of the horror of the American attack and contributed greatly to the Creek disposition to neutrality. The Carolina frontier was saved. In May 1777 in formal peace talks with Carolina, the Lower Cherokees ceded practically all their holdings in South Carolina to the land hungry frontiersmen.

On two later occasions the Cherokees were again briefly to join the war in Carolina. In 1779 when the British swept into the upcountry the Cherokees cooperated with them, only to pull back when hit by Carolina forces. Late in 1781 they attacked Ninety-Six, but were repulsed. The Carolinians again devastated the Lower Towns.

Until 1779 most of the Creeks were held to neutrality. Carolina Indian agent George Galphin who had numerous Creek relatives and friends operated with presents and conferences from Silver Bluff and from Ogeechee Old Town in Georgia to raise up a pro-American neutral party. This party by threatening a Creek civil war if the nation went over to the British kept most of the Creeks out of the war until 1779 when the British occupation of Savannah and move into the backcountry forced Galphin to flee for his life. The Creeks joined the British and to a minor extent ravaged Carolina. Some even participated in the 1780 campaign around Charleston. With the peace they were like the Cherokees forced to yield land to the frontiersmen.

The Catawbas, under the influence of traders and William Henry Drayton went over to the rebel Carolinians. Drayton in 1775 spread among them the story that the British king now demanded four deerskins for goods for which he

formerly asked but two. By mid-July the Catawbas were at
Camden asking for service against the British. The rebels
used Catawbas to track down runaway slaves and to disperse
the Negro companies which loyalists assembled near Charleston. A Catawba company helped repulse the British at
Sullivan's Island in June 1776, and later that year Catawbas
accompanied Major Williamson's campaign against the
Cherokees. In 1779 they fought under General Benjamin
Lincoln in the unsuccessful Georgia campaign. In 1780 they
were with Thomas Sumter's irregulars, and they served
out the war with Nathanael Greene's army. Because of their
loyalty to the successful rebels they were allowed after the
war to remain in their homeland—so that today although
they have liquidated their reservation a few of them are
the only Carolina Indians remaining at the sites where they
were first found at the coming of the English. They are the
last of the Carolina colonial Indian frontier.

Bibliography

Most of the material for this booklet was gathered from documentary sources, primarily from the published *Colonial Records of South Carolina*, edited by A. S. Salley, Jr., J. H. Easterby, and W. L. McDowell, Jr., under the aegis of the South Carolina Archives Commission. While a dip into these works, particularly the Indian Books of South Carolina edited by McDowell, would be rewarding, as they are not available to the general reader, the following books are recommended:

Alden, John R. *John Stuart and the Southern Coloniel Frontier*. Ann Arbor, Mich.: University of Michigan Press, 1944.

Brown, Douglas Summers. *The Catawba Indians*. Columbia, S. C.: University of South Carolina Press, 1966.

Brown, John P. *Old Frontiers*. Kingsport, Tenn.: Southern Publishers, 1938.

Corkran, David H. *The Cherokee Frontier, Conflict and Survival, 1740-62*. Norman, Okla.: University of Oklahoma Press, 1962.

_____. *The Creek Frontier, 1540-1783*. Norman, Okla.: University of Oklahoma Press, 1967.

Crane, Verner W. *The Southern Frontier, 1670-1732*. Ann Arbor, Mich.: University of Michigan Press, 1929; reprinted 1956.

Logan, John Henry. *A History of the Upper Country of South Carolina*. Charleston, S. C.: S. G. Courtenay & Co., 1859.

Meriwether, Robert L. *The Expansion of South Carolina, 1729-1765.* Kingsport, Tenn.: Southern Publishers, 1940.

Milling, Chapman J. *Red Carolinians.* Chapel Hill, N. C.: University of North Carolina Press, 1940; reprinted Columbia, S. C.: University of South Carolina Press, 1970.

Simms, William Gilmore. *The Yemassee, A Romance of Carolina.* Many editions, 1835-1964.

Sirmans, M. Eugene. *Colonial South Carolina, A Political History, 1663-1763.* Chapel Hill, N. C.: University of North Carolina Press, 1965.

Two Carolina Classics . . .

MADAME MARGOT
A Legend of Old Charleston

by JOHN BENNETT   xviii, 110 pages (hardcover)

"A genuine folk-legend which, the author tells us, had its origins in the 'Old Charleston which vanished with the Ancient Regime.' The strange and eerie story is told with a wealth of poetic beauty and grace."   —(London) *Book Exchange*

SKETCHES OF NEGRO LIFE AND HISTORY IN SOUTH CAROLINA
SECOND EDITION

by ASA H. GORDON
Foreword by TOM E. TERRILL
Preface by JOAN L. GORDON   xxiv, 338 pages (paperback)

"The Negro is scarcely known at all to the other races of the world. Contrary to common opinion, he is not fully known to his white neighbors in the South."   —*A. H. Gordon, 1929*

. . . available at the best bookstores